Mushrooms
& Toadstools

Brian Spooner

HarperCollinsPublishers Ltd.
77-85 Fulham Palace Road
London
W6 8JB

The Collins website address is:
www.collins.co.uk

First published in 1996

10 09 08 07 06

10 9 8 7 6 5 4 3

ISBN-13 978 0 00 719150 5
ISBN-10 0 00 719150 2

Edited and designed by D&N Publishing
Colour reproduction by Colourscan, Singapore
Printed and bound by Printing Express Ltd, Hong Kong

INTRODUCTION

Fungi are remarkable organisms. They are present everywhere on earth, in all habitats, and are of enormous biological and ecological importance. Their study is a specialised one, but full of interest and with much yet to discover: it seems clear now that most fungi are still undescribed. Recent estimates suggest that there are over 1.5 million species of fungi, but that less than 5% of them have been described.

True fungi, despite their diversity, have a similar construction, all of them being formed of microscopic, thread-like structures termed hyphae. Aggregations of hyphae, termed mycelium, occur mainly in the soil or in rotten wood, or in other substrates from which they obtain nutrients, and are largely hidden and normally invisible. However, in due course these hyphae develop the fruiting body, the structure such as a mushroom or puffball, which bears the spores and which comes to our attention. Spores are somewhat like the 'seeds' of the fungus; they are dispersed in various ways, and they are able to germinate in suitable conditions to form more hyphae.

Unlike plants, fungi are unable to manufacture their own food. Instead, they must obtain food from other organisms, doing so via the hyphae. Most fungi are saprobes and obtain food only from dead plant or animal matter, although they are often very specific in their requirements, living, for example, only on certain kinds of dead wood or on decaying leaf litter from a particular kind of tree. In contrast, many fungi are parasites, obtaining food directly from living organisms and giving nothing in return. Rusts, smuts and mildews are well-known examples of parasitic fungi. However, many fungi, including many of the common woodland toadstools, are important in developing what are called mycorrhizal associations with plants, especially woody plants. These are intimate and highly specialised associations, the fungi obtaining nutrients from the plant via the roots but in return providing the plant with water and minerals. These are extremely important and widespread relationships, without which the plant is unable to thrive. There is no doubt whatsoever that fungi are of immense ecological significance, and yet there is still so much to learn about them.

HOW TO USE THIS BOOK

This book aims to provide an introduction to the mushrooms and toadstools and other kinds of larger fungi that occur in Britain and northern Europe. As well as a **photograph**, each species is characterised by two **symbols**. The first is a guide to edibility, which is divided into three categories: poisonous, for fungi containing toxins and with known toxic effects; edible; and inedible for all others. It should be emphasised that all fungi, even those regarded as edible, should be well cooked before eating. The second symbol represents the practical grouping to which the fungus belongs; a key to these symbols is given below. A **calendar bar** shows the months in which the fungus fruit-body is normally found. The **'ID Fact File'** provides important descriptive information on the various characters of the species, together with notes on 'Lookalike' species. This latter section is designed to aid identification and to bring to attention possible poisonous lookalikes of edible species, but is not exhaustive.

Key to Symbols

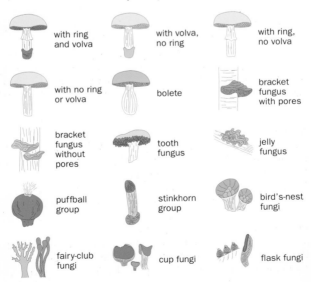

with ring and volva

with volva, no ring

with ring, no volva

with no ring or volva

bolete

bracket fungus with pores

bracket fungus without pores

tooth fungus

jelly fungus

puffball group

stinkhorn group

bird's-nest fungi

fairy-club fungi

cup fungi

flask fungi

LOOKING FOR MUSHROOMS AND TOADSTOOLS

Please remember that fungi should be collected carefully, so that the whole fruitbody, including the stem base in the case of mushrooms and toadstools, is obtained. They should also be collected with minimum disturbance to the habitat and to the fungus mycelium in the soil.

Fungal Habitats

All habitats support fungi of various kinds. In general, different kinds of fungi occur in different habitats, each species being adapted to fill a particular niche so that, for example, the Common Field Mushroom (*Agaricus campestris*) occurs only in grassy places, and the Birch Polypore (*Piptoporus betulinus*) occurs only on dead or dying birch trees. Special habitats such as burnt ground or dung are also rich in fungi. Some species are, of course, less highly specialised than others and are able to grow in a variety of habitats.

Woodlands

Amongst the richest habitats for larger fungi, both deciduous and coniferous woods are ideal places to look for a wide range of species. In general, species found in deciduous woods differ from those found with conifers. Many of the woodland toadstools, for example, form mycorrhizal associations and grow only with certain kinds of tree; similarly, other fungi are parasitic or saprophytic on the wood of certain kinds of tree.

Dunes and Heathlands

Coastal dunes support a distinct group of fungal species, most of them adapted to grow in a particular part of the dune system. The inner fixed dunes support a range fungi different from those found in the unstable outer dunes. Heathlands, on poor, acid soils, also represent a very specialised habitat.

Meadows and Other Kinds of Grassland

The most interesting, and often now the most uncommon, of the grassland fungi are those which occur in unimproved, nutrient-poor meadows. This type of habitat supports a rich community of wild flowers and fungi such as the attractive, bright-coloured Wax-caps, some Fairy-club fungi and Earth-tongues. Regrettably, these habitats are becoming scarce and as a result many of these fungi are now much less common.

Parks and Gardens

These are man-made habitats the soil of which is often nitrogen-rich due to the use of fertilisers. These encourage the growth of a range of fungi, especially the true mushrooms (*Agaricus* species), some of the Ink-caps and Cone-heads, Parasol Mushrooms and Hay-caps amongst many others. Many other species will be found on old rotting stumps and trunks, and many of the grassland species will also occur.

Marshes and Bogs

The fungi of these waterlogged habitats will vary according to the amount of tree cover and whether the soil is acid or alkaline. A range of species grow in *Sphagnum* moss or in wet, decaying leaf litter, and wet ground trees such as willows, alders and birches all support mycorrhizal fungi or species which are parasites or specialists on the decaying wood.

Burnt Ground

After burning, the soil is sterile and also more alkaline. Algae and mosses appear within a few months, as do the first fungi. There follows a succession of species as the site develops and the conditions gradually change. Depending on the habitat in which the fire occurred, different fungi appear in this succession. Common burnt-ground species include Charcoal Scale-head, the Shaggy Bonfire Ink-cap (*Coprinus lagopides*) and a number of different species of Cup-fungi.

Dung

Many fungi are specially adapted to utilise the rich source of nutrients found in animal dung. The dung of herbivores, such as rabbits, horses and cattle, supports the widest variety of species. As on burnt ground, the fungi appear in a distinct succession according to the stage of decay of the dung. While many dung fungi are microscopic, species of Hay-cap, Ink-cap, and larger Cup-fungi, can be found quite commonly.

HOW TO IDENTIFY MUSHROOMS AND TOADSTOOLS

The fungi included in this book are amongst the most readily identifiable of those found in northern Europe. However, the task of identification of fungi is, in general, not an easy one, even amongst the larger species. Correct identification can only be achieved after all the important distinguishing characters of the species have been noted and, indeed, many fungi require careful microscopic examination before an accurate specific identification can be arrived at. This book concentrates on macroscopic characters, i.e. those which can be obtained without the use of a microscope. While these characters may be sufficient for an accurate identification of the main species featured in this book, in some cases the 'Lookalikes' can be satisfactorily distinguished only after microscopic examination.

For any fungus, it is important to note the habitat in which it is found, and what it is growing on, for example rotten wood, soil or dung. Other characters to be noted whilst the specimen is fresh include size, smell, colours of the various parts, the colour changes that may occur when the flesh is broken, the presence and colour of any milk or latex exuded from broken flesh, and, for gill fungi, the presence and kind of any scales or striations on the cap, ring on stem, volva etc. It is also useful to obtain a spore deposit or print from the specimens collected. For gill fungi, remove the stem and place the cap onto a sheet of paper, white for coloured spores but black for white spores. Cover the cap to retain humidity and leave for some hours, preferably overnight, to achieve a good deposit of spores. Other fungi can be treated in a similar way but remember that ascomycetes shoot their spores upwards.

Even though mushrooms have been collected and eaten for centuries, it is important to remember that only relatively few are considered excellent and entirely safe to eat. The edibility of species included in this book is given, although please note that even some normally edible species may cause allergic reactions in some people, and species being eaten for the first time should be taken only in small quantity. Never eat any fungus unless it has been correctly identified by an experienced mycologist, and never mix edible and poisonous species in the collecting basket.

WHAT NEXT?

It is hoped that this book will serve as an introduction to the identification of some of the commoner larger fungi. No single book is or can be comprehensive for such fungi; they are too numerous and their identification is in many cases too critical. Their study therefore requires a range of different books and publications, and for those wishing to make a more detailed study of particular groups will include reference to specialist journals. A selection is given below.

For those who wish to take the subject further, you can join the **British Mycological Society** (www.britmycolsoc.org.uk), that deals with all aspects of mycology. The Society publishes two journals, the *Mycologist*, that carries a range of interesting articles and is aimed particularly at beginners and amateurs, and *Mycological Research*, a specialist scientific journal. The Society organises a range of meetings, including fungus forays, which are invaluable for those wishing to learn more, as the collections of fungi will be identified by experts.

SELECTION OF RECOMMENDED BOOKS

Bon, M. (1987). *The Mushrooms and Toadstools of Britain and North-western Europe*. Hodder & Stoughton.

Courtecuisse, R. and Duhem, B. (1995). *Mushrooms and Toadstools of Britain and Europe*. Collins Field Guide.

Garnweidner, E. (1994) *Mushrooms and Toadstools of Britain and Europe*. Collins Nature Guides.

Pegler, D. N. (1990). *Field Guide to the Mushrooms and Toadstools of Britain and Europe*. Grisewood & Dempsey, Kingfisher Books.

Pegler, D. N. and Spooner, B. M. (1992). *The Mushroom Identifier*. Quintet.

Phillips, R. (1981). *Mushrooms and other Fungi of Great Britain and Europe*. Pan Books.

Buczacki, S. (1989). *Fungi of Britain and Europe*. Collins New Generation Guide.

Spooner, B. and Roberts, P. (2005) *Fungi*. Collins New Naturalist.

AMANITACEAE

False Death Cap
Amanita citrina

ID FACT FILE

CAP: 6–10 cm, convex, pale lemon-yellow, sometimes white, with scale-like patches of veil. Smell of raw potato

STEM: White, smooth, with white or yellowish ring, base swollen with volva forming a rim

GILLS: White, free. Spores white

HABITAT: Deciduous woods

SEASON: Late summer–autumn

LOOKALIKES:
A.virosa is deadly poisonous, always white and has large, sac-like volva. *A. phalloides*, also deadly

A common woodland toadstool, growing especially with oak and beech. Once known as The Napkin, supposedly because its cap resembles a small, round table spread with a cloth. The white form is uncommon but has a similar odour of raw potato. Not poisonous, but unpleasant and should be avoided.

AMANITACEAE

Tawny Grisette
Amanita fulva

ID FACT FILE

CAP: 4–10 cm, convex with raised centre, tawny or orange-brown, edge striate

STEM: Tall, slender, whitish, lacking ring but with sac-like volva

GILLS: Whitish, free. Spores white

HABITAT: Mixed woods, especially with birch

SEASON: Early summer–autumn

LOOKALIKES: Several other ringless *Amanita* species, but these differ in colour and are much less common

A common species, often appearing as early as June. The tawny cap is distinctive. It has a grooved margin but is otherwise smooth and usually free from scale-like remnants of the veil. The species is edible if well cooked, but best avoided. It is the commonest of a group of species known as grisettes, which have a striate cap margin and a slender stem which lacks a ring but is often slightly scaly and has a well-developed volva.

AMANITACEAE

Fly Agaric
Amanita muscaria

ID FACT FILE

CAP: 10–15 cm, convex, scarlet to orange-red with fluffy white scales

STEM: To 20 × 2 cm, white, with ring and bulbous, scaly base

GILLS: White, free. Spores white

HABITAT: Under birch or pine

SEASON: Late summer to late autumn

LOOKALIKES: Unmistakable when fresh

A common species in birch and pine woods, easily recognised in fresh condition. However, the bright red colours may fade to orange-yellow in old, weathered specimens and cap scales may be lost. The veil is fragile, leaving scale-like remains at the stem base. A poisonous species, having hallucinogenic effects; known as the Sacred Mushroom, and of great significance in the folklore of many parts of Europe. It contains ibotenic acid, a weak insecticide, and since medieval times it has been used as a fly killer.

AMANITACEAE

Death Cap
Amanita phalloides

ID FACT FILE

Cap: 5–12 cm, convex, olive-green, radially streaky, smooth or with white veil remnants

Stem: White, with large ring when fresh, bulbous base and large volva

Gills: Free, whitish. Spores white

Habitat: Beech and oak woods

Season: Late summer–late autumn

Lookalikes: False Death Cap is yellowish and lacks large volva. Edible mushrooms have dark gills at maturity

This species is deadly poisonous and is responsible for most deaths from fungal poisoning in Europe. It contains cyclopeptides, cell-damaging compounds, the most dangerous of which are amatoxins. These are not broken down in cooking and cause severe liver damage. Primary symptoms, caused by phallotoxins, appear 8–15 hours after ingestion; those caused by the amatoxins occur later. Appears in oak woods, and can be recognised by the greenish, streaky cap, large ring and volva. White forms also occur.

AMANITACEAE

The Blusher
Amanita rubescens

ID FACT FILE

CAP: 6–12 cm, convex, reddish-brown with grey-brown, scale-like remains of veil

STEM: Whitish or reddish-brown, with ring and swollen, scaly base

GILLS: Free, white, often with red-brown spots. Spores white

HABITAT: Deciduous and coniferous woods

SEASON: Summer–late autumn

LOOKALIKES: *A. excèlsa* and *A. pantherina* lack red tints

Named for the reddish staining which develops when the flesh is cut or bruised, and particularly where eaten by slugs. It is a common woodland toadstool, edible only after thorough cooking. It is poisonous raw, containing haemolytic compounds which cause the breaking up of red blood cells. It is best avoided anyway due to possible confusion with poisonous species such as *A. pantherina*.

AGARICACEAE

Stinking Parasol
Lepiota cristata

ID FACT FILE

CAP: 2–5 cm, bell-shaped, expand-ing, with central boss, whitish with reddish-brown centre and scales. Smell unpleasant

STEM: Slender, whitish to pale brown, with thin, fragile ring

GILLS: Free, white, crowded. Spores white

HABITAT: Woods, parks

SEASON: Summer–late autumn

LOOKALIKES: *L. felina* has blackish scales

One of the commonest of the small *Lepiota* species, occurring throughout Europe, and readily recognised by the unpleasant smell and red-brown scales. It often grows in groups at path edges and amongst leaf litter in woods.

AGARICACEAE

Smooth Parasol
Leucoagaricus leucothites

A frequent grassland species, rather similar in appearance to a common mushroom, and even with a pinkish tinge to the gills, but having white spores. Considered to be edible when cooked, but can cause stomach upsets in some people.

ID FACT FILE

CAP: 6–10 cm, convex to flattened, smooth, whitish

STEM: White, with thin ring in upper part

GILLS: Free, crowded, white to pale pinkish. Spores white

HABITAT: Parks, gardens, etc., in grass

SEASON: Summer–autumn

LOOKALIKES: *Agaricus arvensis* has dark gills and spores

AGARICACEAE

The Parasol
Macrolepiota procera

ID FACT FILE

Cap: 10–25 cm, at first ovoid, expanding to parasol shape, pale buff with brown, soft scales

Stem: Tall, up to 35 cm, slender, with brown snake-like pattern and movable, double, woolly ring

Gills: Free, soft, whitish. Spores white

Habitat: Fields, parks

Season: Summer–autumn

Lookalikes: Shaggy Parasol (p.17) is less slender and without snake-like stem markings. *L. mastoidea* has simple ring

One of the best edible species, common throughout most of Europe and widely distributed in the N hemisphere. It may grow singly or in groups, usually in open parts of woods or in grass. Young fruitbodies are pestle-shaped, but soon expand, leaving a movable ring. The soft cap scales and snake-like markings on the stem are characteristic.

AGARICACEAE

Shaggy Parasol
Macrolepiota rhacodes

ID FACT FILE

Cap: 8–20 cm, at first ovate, expanding, covered in scales, pale buff, darker brown at centre. Flesh reddens when cut

Stem: Whitish, bruising reddish, bulbous at base, with movable ring

Gills: Free, cream. Spores white

Habitat: Hedges, parks, copses

Season: Summer–autumn

Lookalikes: Parasol (p.16); other *Macrolepiota* species, which lack reddening flesh. *Chlorophyllum molybdites* has greenish gills and is poisonous

Common, distinguished amongst similar species by the smooth stem and reddening flesh. Young specimens, before the cap expands, have a characteristic 'drumstick' shape. Grows singly or in groups, in various places including gardens. Although edible, this is inferior to the Parasol, and is indigestible to some people.

TRICHOLOMATACEAE

J	F	M	A	M	J
J	A	S	O	N	D

Honey Fungus
Armillaria mellea

ID FACT FILE

CAP: 4–12 cm, yellowish, with darker centre, scaly

STEM: White or yellowish, with soft, woolly ring, sometimes bulbous below

GILLS: Decurrent, whitish or creamy. Spores white

HABITAT: Woodlands

SEASON: Summer–early winter

LOOKALIKES: Other *Armillaria* species, including *A. tabescens*, which lacks a ring

A common species, usually growing in large tufts. It is a serious parasite of a wide range of woody plants, causing a fibrous white rot, but also fruiting commonly on dead stumps. It spreads by black, bootlace-like rhizomorphs which penetrate beneath bark. The fruitbodies are edible when young. Several similar species are now recognised.

AGARICACEAE

| J | F | M | A | M | J |
| J | A | S | O | N | D |

Saffron Parasol
Cystoderma amianthinum

ID FACT FILE

CAP: 2–4 cm, convex with central boss, bright yellow-brown, powdery, with scaly margin

STEM: 3–5 cm high, whitish and smooth above, yellow-brown and scaly below the distinct ring

GILLS: Adnate, whitish, crowded. Spores white

HABITAT: In moss and short grass, in woods and on heaths

SEASON: Late summer–early winter

LOOKALIKES: *C. granulosum* and *C. jasonis* are deeper in colour

Species of *Cystoderma* can be recognised particularly by the granular or powdery surface to the cap and stem. This is due to the presence of large, globose cells which are developed in chains. This is perhaps the commonest member of the genus, distinguished by the bright ochraceous to yellow-brown colour of the cap and stem.

TRICHOLOMATACEAE

Ringed Knight-cap
Tricholoma cingulatum

ID FACT FILE

CAP: 4–7 cm, convex to flat with slight raised boss, pale grey-brown, felty-scaly

STEM: 5–8 cm high, cylindric, whitish, with woolly ring

GILLS: Sinuate, whitish. Spores white

HABITAT: Damp ground, especially with willow

SEASON: Late summer–autumn

LOOKALIKES: None

One of the few *Tricholoma* species which, because of the well-developed partial veil, have a ring on the stem. It is, therefore, comparatively easy to identify, the greyish cap and occurrence under willows also being characteristic. It is uncommon, but may sometimes occur in large numbers in appropriate habitats.

TRICHOLOMATACEAE

Yellow-brown Knight-cap

Tricholoma fulvum

J	F	M	A	M	J
J	A	S	O	N	D

ID FACT FILE

CAP: 4–8 cm, convex, expanding, chestnut-brown, margin often more yellowish

STEM: To 8 cm high, cap colour, fibrous, with yellow flesh

GILLS: Sinuate, yellowish, soon spotted with brown. Spores white

HABITAT: Woods, often with birch

SEASON: Late summer–autumn

LOOKALIKES: *T. ustale* and relatives have white flesh

One of the most common species of *Tricholoma*, widely distributed and occurring even in montane regions. Identifiable by its yellowish flesh and mealy smell. It grows in mycorrhizal association with birch, but may also be found under conifers. Eaten by some but best avoided as may cause digestive irritation.

TRICHOLOMATACEAE

J	F	M	A	M	J
J	A	S	O	N	D

Sulphur Knight-cap

Tricholoma sulphureum

ID FACT FILE

Cap: 3–8 cm, convex, somewhat expanding, sulphur-yellow, smooth. Odour strong, of gas-tar

Stem: 3–5 cm high, sulphur-yellow

Gills: Adnate-sinuate, sulphur-yellow. Spores white

Habitat: Woods, usually with deciduous trees

Season: Late summer–autumn

Lookalikes: *T. flavovirens* lacks smell and has whitish flesh

A highly distinctive species on account of the yellow colours throughout and the strong, unmistakable odour which is usually likened to gas-tar or coal gas. Various common names reflect its colour or smell; it is also known as Sulphurous Tricholoma and Narcissus Blewit. Occurs with hardwoods and sometimes conifers; widespread but uncommon in Europe.

TRICHOLOMATACEAE

J	F	M	A	M	J
J	A	S	O	N	D

Grey Knight-cap
Tricholoma terreum

ID FACT FILE

CAP: 4–8 cm across, rather conical then expanding, usually with blunt central boss, dark grey or brownish-grey, finely felty-woolly and often slightly scaly. Flesh white, mild, with no distinctive odour

STEM: 5–7 × 1–1.5 cm, whitish or with grey tinge, often slightly clavate at base, smooth, fragile

GILLS: Sinuate, whitish to pale greyish. Spores white

HABITAT: Mostly with conifers

SEASON: Late summer–autumn

LOOKALIKES: Several greyish species differ in less felty cap, in habitat or have a bitter taste. *T. cingulatum*, with greyish, felty cap has a ring on the stem and occurs under willows

Widespread and fairly common in both Europe and North America, usually in coniferous woods, on chalky soils. It is associated mainly with *Picea* and *Pinus*, though will occasionally be found in deciduous woodland. The flesh is mild to the taste when chewed, and this together with the grey, felty cap make the species fairly easy to identify.

TRICHOLOMATACEAE

Plums-and-Custard
Tricholomopsis rutilans

ID FACT FILE

Cap: 4–10 cm, convex, densely covered with small reddish-purple scales on yellow ground

Stem: Cylindric, to 10 cm high, yellowish above, becoming reddish scaly downwards

Gills: Crowded, sinuate, yellowish. Spores creamy-white

Habitat: On rotten coniferous wood

Season: Late summer–late autumn

Lookalikes: None

The common name refers to the characteristic colour of the cap and stem. The species is distinctive and can scarcely be confused with any other. It is frequent throughout most of Europe on coniferous logs and stumps, especially of spruce. A related species, *T. decora*, is golden yellow; it is also on conifers but usually at higher altitudes, and is much less common.

TRICHOLOMATACEAE

J	F	M	A	M	J
J	A	S	O	N	D

Clustered Grey-gill
Lyophyllum decastes

ID FACT FILE

Cap: 4–8 cm, convex, expanding, margin often wavy, brown to grey-brown, smooth

Stem: 4–8 cm high, cylindric or tapered, fibrous, many fused at base, whitish

Gills: Adnate-decurrent, whitish to pale grey. Spores white

Habitat: Woods, parks, often at path edges

Season: Late summer–late autumn

Lookalikes: *L. fumosum*, with darker cap

Widespread in Europe, locally common and occurring in a range of habitats. Previously known as *Tricholoma aggregatum*, this species grows in large tufts of 20 or more caps with stems united at the base. It is variable in colour of cap, and the darker *L. fumosum*, similar in all microscopic characters, is perhaps just a colour form of this species.

TRICHOLOMATACEAE

J	F	M	A	M	J
J	A	S	O	N	D

St George's Mushroom
Calocybe gambosa

ID FACT FILE

Cap: 5–12 cm across, convex, fleshy, whitish to cream or pale tan, smooth; strong floury odour

Stem: Stout, whitish, smooth, lacking ring and volva

Gills: White, sinuate, closely spaced. Spores white

Habitat: Grassy places, woodland edges

Season: Spring, usually late April–late May

Lookalikes: In good condition is unlikely to be confused with other species

An excellent edible species, one of the few to be available in the spring. The popular name is a reference to its appearance on or around St George's Day, 23 April. It is quite common in grassy places, sometimes growing in fairy rings, and the whitish colours and fresh, floury smell make it unmistakable.

TRICHOLOMATACEAE

Broad-gilled Agaric
Megacollybia platyphylla

ID FACT FILE

CAP: 6–11 cm, soon flat, dark grey-brown, radially streaky

STEM: 6–12 cm high, whitish or pale brown, base with white cord-like mycelial strands

GILLS: Adnexed, white, broad, soft, wide-spaced. Spores white

HABITAT: Deciduous woods

SEASON: Late spring–early autumn

LOOKALIKES: None

Common, especially with beech, and recognised by the dark streaky cap and white mycelial cords always present at the stem base. These arise from rotten wood, and the toadstools may be found on old stumps and logs. This species has tough, bitter flesh, and is not edible.

TRICHOLOMATACEAE

Amethyst Deceiver
Laccaria amethystea

ID FACT FILE

CAP: 2–5 cm, convex becoming flattened, slightly scaly, deep violet

STEM: 5–8 cm high, cap colour, tough and fibrous

GILLS: Adnate, thick and distant, violaceous, powdered white at maturity. Spores white

HABITAT: Woods

SEASON: Summer–early winter

LOOKALIKES: None when fresh

J	F	M	A	M	J
J	A	S	O	N	D

Common, often in large groups on the ground in woods, occurring with both deciduous and coniferous trees. Easily recognised when in fresh condition by the violaceous colours throughout, but old and weathered specimens are much paler, more scurfy on the cap and may look very different. Quite a good edible species, also known as the Red Cabbage Fungus.

Abnormal, distorted specimens are quite commonly encountered.

TRICHOLOMATACEAE

J	F	M	A	M	J
J	A	S	O	N	D

The Deceiver

Laccaria laccata

ID FACT FILE

CAP: 2–5 cm, convex to flattened, red-brown or brick, drying paler, slightly scurfy, margin striate, often wavy

STEM: 5–8 cm high, sometimes compressed, cap colour, tough and fibrous

GILLS: Pinkish, thick, distant, white-powdered from spores at maturity. Spores white

HABITAT: Woods

SEASON: Summer –early winter

LOOKALIKES: *L. proxima* is more regular in form and with paler pink gills but distinguished with certainty only on spore characters. *L. bicolor* has a lilac stem base

A very common toadstool, growing singly or in groups in various kinds of woodland. It is very variable in appearance depending on age and conditions, hence the popular name. When dry, the cap can be much more scurfy and is pale to almost whitish although the gills usually retain their colour. The species is edible, but rather tough. The stem is usually rather twisted and compressed.

TRICHOLOMATACEAE

Club-footed Funnel-cap

Clitocybe clavipes

ID FACT FILE

CAP: 3–8 cm, olive-brown to greyish-brown, convex with central boss, soon flattened or slightly depressed, smooth. Flesh whitish

STEM: 3–8 cm high, markedly enlarged towards the base, grey-brown

GILLS: Whitish to creamy-yellow, strongly decurrent. Spores white

HABITAT: Mixed woodlands

SEASON: Autumn

LOOKALIKES: Clouded Agaric (p.31) has greyish cap but is larger and without club-shaped stem. *C. geotropa* is paler and much larger

A common woodland species, especially with birch and beech. The popular name refers to the stem which is distinctly club-shaped. The dark cap and stem contrast with the pale gills, and the species is easy to recognise. The flesh has a pleasant odour, reminiscent of bitter almonds, but despite this the species should be avoided; it causes allergic reactions to some and is suspected of alcohol-related poisoning.

TRICHOLOMATACEAE

J	F	M	A	M	J
J	A	S	O	N	D

Clouded Agaric
Clitocybe nebularis

ID FACT FILE

Cap: 7–15 cm, convex to flattened, fleshy, greyish with whitish bloom. Flesh white

Stem: 7–12 × 2–3 cm, cylindric or slightly enlarged to base, smooth

Gills: Whitish, decurrent, closely spaced. Spores pale pinkish

Habitat: Mixed woods and heathland

Season: September–December

Lookalikes: *C. maxima* is larger and with central boss. *C. alexandri* more yellow-brown and much less common

A large, distinctive species sometimes growing in fairy rings in woods. The greyish cap has a characteristic whitish bloom composed of small tufts of hyphae. The odour of fresh specimens is said to be reminiscent of cottage cheese, and the species was once popularly known as the New Cheese Agaric. Although eaten by some, this fungus should be avoided; it is a stomach irritant to many. It is host occasionally to another toadstool, the rare *Volvariella surrecta*.

TRICHOLOMATACEAE

Blue-green Funnel-cap
Clitocybe odora

ID FACT FILE

CAP: 3–7 cm, convex to flat with incurved margin, smooth, blue-green. Strong odour of aniseed

STEM: 3–5 × 0.5–1 cm, often curved, blue-green, base whitish

GILLS: Paler than cap, slightly decurrent. Spores white

HABITAT: Deciduous and coniferous woods

SEASON: Autumn

LOOKALIKES: In good condition unmistakable on account of colour and odour

An attractive and distinctive species, easily recognised by the blue-green colours and strong aniseed smell, which is retained in dried specimens. A few other *Clitocybe* species have a similar odour, but these are cream or beige, becoming whitish when dry. A good edible species, but mostly used as a flavouring.

TRICHOLOMATACEAE

Giant Funnel-cap
Leucopaxillus giganteus

ID FACT FILE

Cap: 10–30 cm, depressed to funnel-shaped, whitish, downy at margin

Stem: Short, stout, whitish

Gills: Decurrent, crowded, whitish to cream. Spores white

Habitat: Parks, meadows, in grass

Season: Late summer–autumn

Lookalikes: *C. geotropa* is taller, with central boss

Frequent in various grassland habitats. The large, whitish, short-stalked fruitbodies are often found growing in fairy rings and are said to kill the grass within the ring. It is one of the largest toadstools, not easily mistaken when in good condition. Although edible by most people, it produces unpleasant symptoms in some.

TRICHOLOMATACEAE

Buttercap
Collybia butyracea

ID FACT FILE

CAP: 3–7 cm, moist, with central boss, dark brown, becoming paler on drying except at centre

STEM: Fibrous, finely grooved, thicker towards the base, cap colour

GILLS: White, crowded, adnexed. Spores white

HABITAT: Mixed woods, on acid soils

SEASON: Autumn–early winter

LOOKALIKES: *C. distorta* and *C. prolixa*, much rarer, have more slender stem and lack dark umbo

Somewhat variable in colour but the damp, rather greasy feel to the cap and its dark centre are characteristic. The fibrous stem, enlarged towards the base, is also typical, and the colour contrast between the stem and gills is distinctive. A common woodland species, often continuing to be found after the first frosts. A pale form which occurs on richer soils is known as var. *asema*.

TRICHOLOMATACEAE

J	F	M	A	M	J
J	A	S	O	N	D

Wood Tough-shank
Collybia dryophila

ID FACT FILE

CAP: 3–5 cm, convex to flattened, smooth, usually pale yellowish-orange

STEM: Cap colour or paler, thicker at the base, smooth, tough

GILLS: White or cream, adnexed. Spores white

HABITAT: Deciduous or mixed woods, and heaths

SEASON: Late spring to late autumn

LOOKALIKES: *C. distorta*, with pines, usually larger and more deeply coloured and with more grooved stem. *C. ocior* has yellow gills

A very common species throughout Europe. It is found in various kinds of woodland, and is somewhat variable particularly with regard to colour of the cap which ranges from whitish to pale tan or orange-yellow. Often growing in groups, it may appear as early as late spring and has a long fruiting period. This is an edible species, but it has thin, fibrous flesh and is not greatly valued from this point of view.

TRICHOLOMATACEAE

Spindle Shank
Collybia fusipes

ID FACT FILE

CAP: 3–7 cm, convex, smooth, deep red-brown

STEM: Rooting, swollen at centre and tapered at base, fibrous, twisted

GILLS: Thick, rather distant, whitish with red-brown spots. Spores white

HABITAT: Base of deciduous trees or stumps, especially oak

SEASON: Summer –autumn

LOOKALIKES: Unmistakable when in good condition

A common and distinctive species which is aptly named for its markedly spindle-shaped stem. It grows in large tufts, usually at the base of oak and sweet chestnut trees, or growing from the roots. The red-brown colour, spindle-shaped, grooved and often twisted stem and the habitat make this species highly distinctive. Edible, but not much valued owing to the tough, fibrous flesh.

TRICHOLOMATACEAE

J	F	M	A	M	J
J	A	S	O	N	D

Spotted Tough-shank

Collybia maculata

ID FACT FILE

Cap: 4–9 cm, convex to flattened, smooth, white with red-brown spots, occasionally entirely red-brown. Tough, fibrous flesh makes it inedible

Stem: Tall, fibrous, tough, rooting

Gills: Crowded, white or red-brown spotted, free. Spores pale pinkish

Habitat: Deciduous and coniferous woodland

Season: Late summer–autumn

Lookalikes: Spindle Shank (p.36) also red-brown spotted, but has spindle-shaped stem and grows in tufts

This is one of the largest of the *Collybia* species, very common in leaf litter in woodland, and often forming fairy rings. It is basically a white species, but with variable development on all parts of red-brown spots, hence the common name. It is not poisonous but, like other *Collybia* species, it has tough, fibrous flesh and is not recommended for eating.

TRICHOLOMATACEAE

Wood Woolly-foot

Collybia peronata

ID FACT FILE

CAP: 3–6 cm, pale yellow-brown, convex to flattened. Taste peppery

STEM: 4–7 cm × 3–6 mm, pale yellowish, lower part conspicuously hairy, binding leaf litter

GILLS: Yellowish, widely spaced, adnexed. Spores white

HABITAT: Deciduous and coniferous woods

SEASON: Late summer–late autumn

LOOKALIKES: *C. alkalivirens* and *C. fuscopurpure a* have much darker reddish-brown colours and mild taste, and are comparatively rare

A very common woodland toadstool, growing with various trees, but especially with beech, often binding the leaf litter by abundant mycelium. It is somewhat variable, but usually readily recognisable by the woolly stem base and yellowish stem. The flesh is tough and pliant, and has a distinct peppery taste when chewed for a while. Dried fruitbodies are used as a flavouring in parts of Europe, but the species is generally not recommended for eating.

TRICHOLOMATACEAE

Porcelain Fungus
Oudemansiella mucida

ID FACT FILE

Cap: 3–8 cm, convex, whitish, slimy, margin striate

Stem: To 6 cm high, slender, with swollen base, whitish, with ring

Gills: Adnate or adnexed, distant, white. Spores white

Habitat: Dead trunks and branches, usually of beech

Season: Late summer–autumn

Lookalikes: None

A common, attractive and distinctive species, growing in clumps mostly on dead beech wood; it is sometimes known also as Beech Tuft or Poached Egg Fungus. The slimy white, translucent cap and ringed stem are unmistakable. An antiobiotic, known as mucidin, can be obtained from the mycelium of this species, and acts against fungi of the skin. The species is edible after washing to remove the slime from the cap, but is not recommended.

TRICHOLOMATACEAE

Rooting Shank
Oudemansiella radicata

ID FACT FILE

CAP: 3–8 cm, convex to flattened, brown, radially wrinkled, slimy when wet

STEM: Tall, pale brown, striate, tapered upwards and with long, rooting base

GILLS: Adnexed, white, often with brown edge, soft. Spores white

HABITAT: Woods, on rotten stumps and buried wood

SEASON: Summer–late autumn

LOOKALIKES: *O. longipes* has dry, velvety cap and stem

A common species of deciduous woods. The fruitbodies spring from rotten wood and have a distinctive rooting base which is occasionally developed to extreme length. That of a specimen from Leigh Woods, Bristol, growing in a rotten birch trunk was recently measured as over 60 cm long! An edible species, but with little to recommend it.

TRICHOLOMATACEAE

Velvet Shank
Flammulina velutipes

ID FACT FILE

CAP: 2–8 cm, convex, expanding, yellow-orange, smooth

STEM: Yellowish above, otherwise dark brown and distinctly velvety, usually curved

GILLS: Adnexed, pale yellow. Spores white

HABITAT: Decaying decidous trees, especially elm

SEASON: Mostly early–mid-winter

LOOKALIKES: None; the dark, velvety stem and late season make it distinctive

Sometimes known as the Winter Toadstool, this appears late in the season, often after the first frosts, and can be found throughout the winter. It grows in tufts on various deciduous trees, but is most frequent on dead elms, causing a white rot of the sapwood. The dark brown velvety stem and yellow-orange cap are distinctive, and the species is edible.

TRICHOLOMATACEAE

J	F	M	A	M	J
J	A	S	O	N	D

Horse-hair Fungus
Marasmius androsaceus

ID FACT FILE

Cap: 0.5–1 cm, convex to flattened, reddish-brown, radially striate. Flesh thin

Stem: Thin, wiry, blackish, smooth, shining

Gills: Adnate, cap colour. Spores white

Habitat: On heather stems and conifer needles

Season: Late summer–autumn

Lookalikes: *Micromphale perforans*, on spruce needles, has thicker stem and cabbage smell. *Marasmius bulliardii* and *M. rotula* have paler caps and gills attached to a collar

A common and distinctive species. The thin blackish stem resembles a horse-hair, hence the popular name, and usually arises from thin, black rhizoids which grow over the substrate and also resemble horsehairs. It grows as a parasite on heather, and as a saprophyte on conifer needles and other leaf litter. The structure of the cap skin in this species is unusual, more akin to that of the related genus *Marasmiellus*. For this reason it has been recently referred to a new genus *Setulipes*.

TRICHOLOMATACEAE

J	F	M	A	M	J
J	A	S	O	N	D

Fairy Ring Champignon
Marasmius oreades

ID FACT FILE

CAP: 2–5 cm, creamy-buff when dry, convex, with broad central boss, smooth

STEM: To 8 cm high, pale buff, tough, dry

GILLS: Free to adnexed, rather distant, whitish to pale buff. Spores white

HABITAT: Grassland, in fairy rings

SEASON: Late spring–autumn

LOOKALIKES: Some *Collybia* species may be similar, but grow in woods

The commonest of the fairy-ring formers in grassland. Rings expand slowly over many years and can be recognised by the lush growth of grass at their inner edge. Toadstools appear in a zone just outside the lush grass. Extensive folklore originates from times when their existence was unexplained and attributed to the supernatural. It is said that the fairies danced in a ring on a summer evening, toadstools grew in their tracks and were used as seats by the tired elves. A good edible species, which also dries well, but take care not to gather with it poisonous *Clitocybe* species which can occur in similar places.

TRICHOLOMATACEAE

Little Wheel Toadstool
Marasmius rotula

J	F	M	A	M	J
J	A	S	O	N	D

ID FACT FILE

Cap: 0.5–1.5 cm, convex with centre umbilicate, whitish, radially grooved

Stem: Slender, tough, blackish or red-brown, smooth, shining

Gills: Distant, attached to collar at stem apex. Spores white

Habitat: On twigs, roots, etc. in woods

Season: Late summer–autumn

Lookalikes: *M. bulliardii* is smaller, with dark brown centre, and grows on leaves

The gills of this species are attached to a collar around the top of the stem, giving the appearance of spokes radiating from the hub of a wheel, hence the common name. The cap, whitish, depressed at the centre and radially grooved, resembles a miniature parachute. This is a common species, readily recognised by the distinctive characters noted.

TRICHOLOMATACEAE

Yellow-stemmed Bonnet-cap
Mycena epipterygia

J	F	M	A	M	J
J	A	S	O	N	D

ID FACT FILE

CAP: 1–2 cm across, bell-shaped, with scalloped margin, striate, slimy, pale grey to yellowish

STEM: Long, slender, to 8 cm high, lemon yellow to greenish, slimy

GILLS: Adnate, whitish, edge gelatinous. Spores white

HABITAT: Coniferous woods, heaths, amongst litter

SEASON: Summer–autumn

LOOKALIKES: None; size, separable gelatinous pellicle and gill edge diagnostic

A generally common species in Europe, but somewhat variable in colour. It has a slimy, often bright lemon-yellow stem, and the cap is also slimy, having a gelatinous skin or pellicle which can be easily peeled off. One interesting feature of this species is that the gills and mycelium are reported to be faintly luminous when carefully examined in the dark.

TRICHOLOMATACEAE

J	F	M	A	M	J
J	A	S	O	N	D

Yellow-white Bonnet-cap

Mycena flavoalba

ID FACT FILE

CAP: 1–1.5 cm, conical, expanding, striate, whitish to cream or pale yellow, often with brighter yellow centre

STEM: To 4 cm high, slender, white or pale yellowish

GILLS: Adnate, white, widely spaced. Spores white

HABITAT: In grass, sometimes in woods

SEASON: Summer–early winter

LOOKALIKES: Several whitish species referred to *Hemimycena*

A small but fairly common species, occurring most often in grassland but occasionally amongst leaf litter in woods. It often grows in groups, and is usually recognisable by the colour of the cap. However, this is variable and the yellow tints may be lacking. In old specimens, the cap expands to leave a central boss, and the margin is often upturned. Edible, but far too small and fragile to be worthwhile.

TRICHOLOMATACEAE

Rooting Bonnet-cap
Mycena galericulata

ID FACT FILE

CAP: 2–5 cm, conical, expanding, with central boss, grey-brown or paler, margin striate

STEM: To 10 cm high, cap colour, tough, base hairy, rooting

GILLS: Adnate, white, often becoming pinkish with age, connected by veins. Spores white

HABITAT: On rotten deciduous logs and stumps, in clumps

SEASON: Early spring–early winter

LOOKALIKES: *M. inclinata*, with red-brown stem; *M. maculata*, with red-brown cap and stem and often red-brown spotted gills; *M. polygramma*

A very common species, and one of the largest of the Bonnet-caps, growing in tufts on rotten logs and stumps. The stems are downy below and usually become fused together. It is variable in colour, and also in cap striation, but the habit and rooting stem are characteristic. The gills are often pinkish with age and much intervened, but these characters can be found in other species also.

TRICHOLOMATACEAE

Milk-drop Bonnet-cap
Mycena galopus

ID FACT FILE

CAP: 1–2 cm, bell-shaped or convex, greyish or white.

STEM: Slender, smooth, often downy at the base, cap colour, exuding milky droplets when broken

GILLS: Adnexed, whitish. Spores white

HABITAT: In leaf and needle litter in woods; sometimes on wood

SEASON: Summer–autumn

LOOKALIKES: Several small *Mycena* species, but these lack milky fluid

Very common. There are two colour forms of this species, both of which exude white, milky droplets from the broken stem. The typical greyish form is common in woodland litter, the white form (var. *alba*) less so. A dark, blackish form often found on peaty or burnt soil is frequently known as *M. leucogala* but is now considered to be another variety of *M. galopus*. The species is not poisonous, but is too small and fragile for eating.

TRICHOLOMATACEAE

| J | F | M | A | M | J |
| J | A | S | O | N | D |

Oak Bonnet-cap
Mycena inclinata

ID FACT FILE

Cap: 1.5–3 cm across, conical, expanding, red-brown, striate, margin slightly toothed at first. Smell unpleasant, rancid-mealy

Stem: Slender, 4–10 cm high, reddish-brown below pale apex

Gills: Adnate, whitish then often pale flesh-colour. Spores white

Habitat: On rotten logs and stumps, usually of oak, in tufts

Season: Autumn–early winter

Lookalikes: Rooting Bonnet-cap (p.47) lacks red-brown colours. *M. maculata* lacks smell. *M. renati* lacks smell, and stem is more uniformly yellow

A widespread and fairly common species which can be distinguished by the tough, two-coloured stem distinctly reddish-brown towards the base, and by the characteristic odour. It usually grows in dense tufts, for which reason it is sometimes known as the Gregarious Elf-cap. It occurs mostly on oak but rarely on other hardwood trees. The species is regarded as inedible, being tough and unpleasant to the taste.

TRICHOLOMATACEAE

Nitrous Bonnet-cap

Mycena leptocephala

ID FACT FILE

Cap: 1–2 cm, bell-shaped, grey with paler margin, striate. Strong nitrous odour

Stem: Slender, to 6 cm high, pale grey-brown, smooth

Gills: Adnexed, pale grey. Spores white

Habitat: On wood or soil in grass, in parks, woods etc.

Season: Summer–autumn

Lookalikes: *M. aetites* lacks nitrous smell. *M. stipata* grows in clusters on rotten coniferous wood

A common species, especially amongst leaf-litter and often on wood. A strong nitrous odour is characteristic of this species, but also of several others. The slender, solitary or gregarious but non-tufted fruitbodies aid the recognition of *M. leptocephala*. The species has sometimes been referred to as *M. ammoniaca*.

TRICHOLOMATACEAE

J	F	M	A	M	J
J	A	S	O	N	D

Lawn Bonnet-cap
Mycena olivaceomarginata

ID FACT FILE

CAP: 1–2 cm, conical, honey-coloured or olive-yellow, striate at margin

STEM: Slender, cap colour, apex paler, smooth

GILLS: Adnate, whitish to pale grey with yellow-brown or olive edge. Spores white

HABITAT: In grass

SEASON: Autumn

LOOKALIKES: *M. citrinomarginata* is more brightly coloured, gill edge yellow

Frequent, growing in troops on lawns and in other grassy places sometimes in company with other similar species. It is readily distinguished from these by the coloured gill edge which is best observed using a hand lens. This species was previously known as *M. avenacea*.

TRICHOLOMATACEAE

Lilac Bonnet-cap
Mycena pura

ID FACT FILE

CAP: 2–5 cm, conical, expanding to almost flat, lilac or pinkish, margin striate. Odour of radish

STEM: To 6 cm high, cap colour, smooth, base white-woolly

GILLS: Adnate or slightly decurrent, pale pinkish. Spores white

HABITAT: In woods

SEASON: Late summer–autumn

LOOKALIKES: *M. pelianthina* has dark gill edge

Common in both coniferous and deciduous woods throughout Europe, growing on the ground amongst leaf litter. Variable in colour; violaceous and white forms also occur, but all have a strong radish-like smell. This species contains toxins of the indole group which can cause hallucinations.

TRICHOLOMATACEAE

Bleeding Bonnet-cap
Mycena sanguinolenta

ID FACT FILE

CAP: 0.5–1.5 cm, bell-shaped, expanding, with central boss, red-brown, centre darker, margin striate

STEM: Slender, reddish, exuding reddish juice when broken

GILLS: Adnate, tinted cap colour, edge dark red. Spores white

HABITAT: In woods, on rotten twigs and bark, sometimes on the ground

SEASON: Autumn

LOOKALIKES: *M. haematopus* has red juice but is much more robust, lacks dark gill edge and grows on logs and stumps

A common species throughout Europe, usually growing singly or in small groups amongst leaf litter in woods. Fruitbodies often appear to be growing on the ground but in fact spring from buried wood. The species is distinguished by the watery red juice, coloured gill edge and slender stature.

TRICHOLOMATACEAE

Turf Navel-cap
Omphalina ericetorum

ID FACT FILE

Cap: 1–3 cm across, yellow-buff, striate, convex then depressed to funnel-shaped

Stem: 1–2.5 cm high, slender, sometimes curved, cap colour, often lilac above

Gills: Deeply decurrent, cream to pale yellowish-buff. Spores white

Habitat: Heath-land and wood-land on damp, acid soil, amongst moss

Season: All year, especially late spring–autumn

Lookalikes: *O. pyxidata* is more reddish-brown

Common in most of Europe, even into sub-alpine regions, sometimes growing in swarms on damp, heathy ground. This and some related species form an association with a green alga and are regarded as lichenised. The alga forms dark green, gelatinous pustules, known as *Botrydina vulgaris*, which are often common on damp, peaty soil.

TRICHOLOMATACEAE

Orange Navel-cap
Rickenella fibula

ID FACT FILE

CAP: 0.5–1 cm, convex with depressed centre, orange-yellow

STEM: Slender, to 4 cm high, pale orange, smooth

GILLS: Deeply decurrent, whitish. Spores white

HABITAT: In moss and grass

SEASON: Summer–autumn

LOOKALIKES: *R. swartzii* is paler, with dark centre to cap

Common in damp places amongst moss, usually in woods but also in meadows. It often grows with *R. swartzii*, of which it was once considered a variety. Both species have previously been placed in *Omphalina*, owing to the decurrent gills, and in *Mycena*, but they have microscopic characters which are unlike species of those genera.

TRICHOLOMATACEAE

| J | F | M | A | M | J |
| J | A | S | O | N | D |

Pick-a-back Toadstool
Asterophora lycoperdoides

ID FACT FILE

Cap: 1–2 cm, hemispherical or convex, brownish, powdery.

Stem: Short, cylindric, lacking ring

Gills: Thick, adnate, rudimentary

Habitat: On old fruitbodies, usually of blackening species of *Russula*

Season: Late summer–autumn

Lookalikes: *A. parasitica* is more slender and has a smooth cap

An unusual and distinctive species which occurs almost always on decaying fruitbodies of Blackening Russule (p.67) more rarely on other species of *Russula* and *Lactarius*. The cap is markedly powdery owing to the production of special spores called chlamydospores. Gills are thick and soft, and usually poorly developed. Common, particularly in wet seasons.

HYGROPHORACEAE

Blackening Wax-cap
Hygrocybe conica

ID FACT FILE

CAP: 1.5–4 cm wide, conical, smooth, silky, reddish-orange, blackening

STEM: To 8 cm high, yellowish or orange, blackening

GILLS: Free to adnexed, white to pale yellow, blackening. Spores white

HABITAT: Grassy places, also on dunes

SEASON: Mid-summer–late autumn

LOOKALIKES: *H. conicoides*, with obtuse, reddish cap and pinkish-red gills, in dunes

A common and readily recognised wax-cap, occurring in unimproved pastures and meadows, even into alpine regions. The conical cap and blackening of the flesh when bruised or with age are characteristic. *Hygrocybe nigrescens*, separated by many authors, is now usually considered a synonym. Although not regarded as edible, this species has been used in the past in folk medicine.

HYGROPHORACEAE

Meadow Wax-cap
Hygrocybe pratensis

ID FACT FILE

CAP: 4–8 cm across, with raised boss, fleshy, pale orange-buff, smooth, dry

STEM: 3–5 × 1–1.5 cm, paler than cap, slightly tapered to base

GILLS: Decurrent, wide-spaced, paler than cap. Spores white

HABITAT: Meadows and pastures

SEASON: Autumn

LOOKALIKES: *H. nemoreus*, similar in colour but more slender and found in woods

Fairly common, usually occurring in meadows, or occasionally on heaths. This is a good edible species which is best appreciated if cooked by itself. In its typical form it is unlikely to be confused with any other species. However, there is also an uncommon white form which may be similar to *H. virginea* in appearance. The species is common in Europe, and is sometimes also known as Buff Caps.

HYGROPHORACEAE

Parrot Wax-cap
Hygrocybe psittacina

ID FACT FILE

Cap: 2–4 cm, slimy, bell-shaped, expanding, yellow to orange, covered with blue-green gluten

Stem: Slimy, green, becoming yellow below

Gills: Adnate, thick, pale yellow, green in part. Spores white

Habitat: In grass, mostly in pastures, less often in woods

Season: Late summer–early winter

Lookalikes: None; green colours are diagnostic

An attractive but very slimy species, easily recognised by the distinctive green and yellow colours which can occur in all parts, and to which the common name refers. The green colour may fade, but persists at the stem apex even in old specimens. The species occurs throughout Europe in poor meadows and open areas in woods, but is apparently declining, like many wax-caps, through loss and degradation of habitats.

HYGROPHORACEAE

Satin-white Wax-cap

Hygrocybe virginea

ID FACT FILE

Cap: 1–4 cm, convex, with central boss, smooth, white or pale cream, greasy

Stem: 3–6 cm high, cylindric, whitish, smooth

Gills: Decurrent, wide-spaced, white. Spores white

Habitat: In grass of meadows, lawns, etc.

Season: Autumn

Lookalikes: *H. russocoriaceus* smells strongly of 'Russian leather'; some white *Clitocybe* species, which are poisonous

One of the commonest of the grassland wax-caps, preferring meadows on clay soil and occurring even into alpine regions. *Hygrocybe nivea*, separated on microscopic characters by some authors, is now usually regarded as a synonym. Easily recognised by the ivory-white cap and lack of smell, and sometimes growing in profusion. It is an edible species, highly recommended by some.

HYGROPHORACEAE

Herald of the Winter
Hygrophorus hypothejus

ID FACT FILE

CAP: 3–6 cm across, convex then flattened, slimy, dark olive-brown becoming paler. Flesh yellowish

STEM: 4–8 cm high, yellowish, slimy, usually tapered, with ring-like zone near the top

GILLS: Decurrent, yellowish, thick and rather distant. Spores white

HABITAT: With pines on acid soil

SEASON: Late autumn–early winter

LOOKALIKES: Season and colours are distinctive

The species occurs from late autumn, often appearing after the first frosts, hence the popular name. It is quite common in pine woodland, often growing in troops, and can usually be easily recognised by its late season, the dark, olive-brown, slimy cap and yellowish flesh. The species is edible, but is said to be best when dried, when it has a crisp, pleasant texture and makes an ideal snack.

RUSSULACEAE

| J | F | M | A | M | J |
| J | A | S | O | N | D |

Birch Russule
Russula betularum

ID FACT FILE

CAP: 2–5 cm across, convex to flattened, reddish-pink then pale pink to whitish. Margin grooved. Flesh thin, fragile, hot to taste

STEM: White, slightly thicker to base

GILLS: Almost free, white. Spores white

HABITAT: Under birches in damp woodland

SEASON: Autumn

LOOKALIKES: *R. emeticella*, usually with darker cap, and pale yellow gills

One of the more distinctive of the *Russula* species, owing to the pale pink, sometimes almost whitish cap. Unlike most species of *Russula*, the cap skin, or cuticle, can be completely peeled off. It is a common species of damp birch woodland. Like other acrid-tasting *Russula* species, it is slightly poisonous, and worthless from the culinary point of view. It should never be eaten raw, though is safe if well cooked.

RUSSULACEAE

| J | F | M | A | M | J |
| J | A | S | O | N | D |

The Charcoal Burner
Russula cyanoxantha

ID FACT FILE

CAP: 5–12 cm, convex to flattened, smooth, lilac to purple, with grey, yellow or olive tints. Taste mild

STEM: 4–7 × 1.5–2 cm, white or with purple flush

GILLS: Adnate, white, flexible, sometimes forked. Spores white

HABITAT: Deciduous woodland, mostly with beech

SEASON: Early summer–autumn

LOOKALIKES: Several may look similar, but lack of salmon reaction in stem when rubbed with iron salts is distinctive

A common species, but very variable with regard to cap colour. Lilac is usually present, and this together with the mild taste, white spores and habitat should make identification easy. However, there is a green form which can closely resemble *R. heterophylla*. Unlike most species the stem, when rubbed with iron salts, does not give a salmon reaction. It is usually considered a good edible species, but should be well cooked first.

RUSSULACEAE

J	F	M	A	M	J
J	A	S	O	N	D

The Sickener
Russula emetica

ID FACT FILE

CAP: 4–10 cm, convex to flattened, bright red or scarlet, smooth. Taste very hot

STEM: 3–8 × 1–1.5 cm, pure white, thicker to base, fragile

GILLS: Adnate, white to pale cream, rather distant. Spores white

HABITAT: Under pines

SEASON: Summer–late autumn

LOOKALIKES: *R. mairei* is very similar, but is found under beech

A common species of pine woods, occurring throughout Europe. The scarlet cap, white stem and gills, and very hot, acrid taste are characteristic, but there are several red-capped *Russula* species and identification can be very difficult. This species, like others with an acrid taste, is inedible, being a stomach irritant, and causes sickness if eaten raw.

RUSSULACEAE

J	F	M	A	M	J
J	A	S	O	N	D

Straw-coloured Russule
Russula fellea

This species is sometimes known as the Geranium-scented *Russula*, but the smell is more reminiscent of rhubarb. It can be recognised by the smell and by the straw-yellow colour of all parts. It is a fairly common species that grows mostly with beech and can often be found in company with *R. mairei* which has a red cap, and white gills and stem.

ID FACT FILE

CAP: 4–8 cm, convex to flattened, straw-yellow. Taste hot. Odour fruity

STEM: 4–7 × 1–1.5 cm, cap colour

GILLS: Adnate, pale straw, crowded. Spores pale cream

HABITAT: Deciduous woods, especially with beech

SEASON: Summer –late autumn

LOOKALIKES: Common Yellow Russule (p.68) has brighter yellow cap, whitish gills and white to greyish stem

RUSSULACEAE

J	F	M	A	M	J
J	A	S	O	N	D

Fragile Russule
Russula fragilis

ID FACT FILE

CAP: 2–6 cm, convex to flattened or depressed, purplish, often with green and violet tints, fragile. Taste very hot

STEM: 2–6 × 0.5–1.5 cm, white, fragile

GILLS: Adnexed, white, with edges minutely irregularly toothed (use hand lens). Spores white

HABITAT: Woods, especially with oak and birch

SEASON: Summer –autumn

LOOKALIKES: *R. gracillima*, usually paler, has cream spores and pinkish stem

This species is very variable in colour, but can be recognised by the serrated edge to the gills which is characteristic. For this reason it is also known as the Tooth-gill Russule. It is a common woodland species, found throughout Europe and occurring with both deciduous trees and conifers. Like other species with an acrid taste, it is a stomach irritant which is best avoided and should certainly never be eaten raw.

RUSSULACEAE

| J | F | M | A | M | J |
| J | A | S | O | N | D |

Blackening Russule
Russula nigricans

ID FACT FILE

Cap: 6–18 cm, convex, then depressed at centre, off-white becoming dark brown to blackish. Flesh reddening. Taste slowly hot

Stem: 3–8 × 1–3 cm, white to brownish or black

Gills: Adnate, cream to straw, then blackening, thick, distant. Spores white

Habitat: Woods

Season: Late summer–late autumn

Lookalikes: *R. densifolia* has much more crowded gills

A common woodland species, easily recognised by the large, robust fruitbodies which have thick, wide-spaced gills and flesh which reddens at first and becomes black with age. Old and rotting fruitbodies are commonly host to Pick-a-back Toadstool (p.56) and the closely related *Asterophora parasitica*, and also to the small white *Microcollybia tuberosa* whose fruitbodies develop from small reddish-brown sclerotia, developed on the rotting flesh.

RUSSULACEAE

Common Yellow Russule

Russula ochroleuca

ID FACT FILE

CAP: 4–10 cm, convex to flattened, ochre-yellow, margin slightly striate

STEM: 4–7 × 1–2 cm, white then greying, often veined

GILLS: Adnexed, whitish to cream. Spores white to pale cream

HABITAT: Woods, usually with deciduous trees

SEASON: Late summer–late autumn

LOOKALIKES: *R. claroflava* is brighter yellow and has yellowish gills; *R. lutea* has egg-yellow gills

One of the commonest *Russula* species, occurring in various types of woodland. The yellow cap becomes paler with age and is slightly slimy in wet conditions. The grey colour in the stem develops with age, especially when wet, and is characteristic. The species has a mild or slightly hot taste and can be eaten if well cooked.

RUSSULACEAE

Purple Pine Russule
Russula sardonia

ID FACT FILE

Cap: 4–10 cm, convex, expanding, purplish-red. Taste very hot

Stem: 4–7 × 1–2 cm, usually greyish-lilac

Gills: Adnate, yellowish. Spores cream

Habitat: Under pines on acid soil

Season: Late summer–late autumn

Lookalikes: *R. queletii* is similar in colour but with cream gills

An attractive species, frequent in pine woods throughout Europe. The cap colour varies somewhat and is sometimes more purple, or with greenish or yellow tints. The stem may occasionally be white. A drop of ammonia on the gills or flesh produces a rose colour, diagnostic of the species. It has a very hot, acrid taste and is inedible.

RUSSULACEAE

Curry-scented Milk-cap
Lactarius camphoratus

ID FACT FILE

CAP: 2–8 cm,
convex then
flattened or
depressed, red-
brown, smooth,
margin striate.
Curry-like smell
when drying.
Taste mild

STEM: To 5 cm
high, cap colour

GILLS: Decurrent,
pale reddish-
brown. Spores
whitish

HABITAT: Woods,
mainly with pine

SEASON: Late
summer–late
autumn

LOOKALIKES: *L.
serifluus* has a
similar smell but
is dull brown

A fairly common species usually occurring in
coniferous woodland, and distinguished by the
colour and strong curry-like odour of its drying
fruitbodies. It is an edible species, sometimes
used as a flavouring when dried and powdered.
The flesh exudes a thin, watery milk when
broken.

RUSSULACEAE

Spruce Milk-cap
Lactarius deliciosus

ID FACT FILE

CAP: 4–9 cm, zoned, orange-red, staining greenish, convex to depressed. Flesh yellowish to carrot colour, later grey-green. Taste mild

STEM: 3–6 cm high, pale, marked with orange spots, often becoming greenish

GILLS: Adnate–decurrent, pale orange, greenish when bruised. Spores pale ochre

HABITAT: Under pine and spruce

SEASON: Summer –late autumn

LOOKALIKES: *L. deterrimus*, milk turns purplish and flesh has more green staining. *L. sanguifluus* has blood-red milk

Fairly common and a good edible species, long esteemed in parts of Europe, and said to be represented in the frescoes of Herculaneum and Pompeii. It has a mild, pleasant taste and can be fried or grilled or used in soups and stews. It is also known as the Orange-milk Mushroom and Saffron Milk-cap.

RUSSULACEAE

Coconut Milk-cap

Lactarius glyciosmus

ID FACT FILE

CAP: 3–6 cm, greyish-lilac, convex, expanding. Milk white. Smell of dried coconut. Taste mild

STEM: To 7 cm high, paler than cap, smooth

GILLS: Adnate-decurrent, pale greyish-lilac. Spores cream

HABITAT: Woods, mainly with birch

SEASON: Autumn

LOOKALIKES: *L. mammosus* also smells of coconut but has dark brown cap and grows under conifers

Widespread in Europe, and common in some areas, growing in groups especially in birch woodland. It is easily recognised by the coconut smell and pale, rather greyish cap. An edible species, though said to have a bitter taste and not much recommended.

RUSSULACEAE

J	F	M	A	M	J
J	A	S	O	N	D

Liver Milk-cap

Lactarius hepaticus

ID FACT FILE

CAP: 3–6 cm, convex or depressed at centre, dark brown, drying paler. Milk white, turning yellow on handkerchief. Taste hot

STEM: to 5 cm high, cap colour

GILLS: Adnate-decurrent, ochraceous. Spores whitish

HABITAT: Under pine and spruce

SEASON: Autumn

LOOKALIKES:
L. britannicus (in Britain) is more reddish-orange

Common, recognised by the liver-coloured cap and yellowing milk, which is seen best as it dries on a handkerchief. *Lactarius tabidus* is another common species which has yellowing milk, but it grows in deciduous woods and has a much paler cap.

RUSSULACEAE

Oak Milk-cap
Lactarius quietus

ID FACT FILE

CAP: 5–8 cm, convex to depressed, dull red-brown faintly zoned with darker spots. Taste mild; odour oily. Milk white, unchanging

STEM: 3–7 cm, cap colour, slightly streaky, spongy

GILLS: Adnate-decurrent, paler than cap. Spores white

HABITAT: Oak woods

SEASON: Late summer–autumn

LOOKALIKES: *L. chrysorrheus* may look similar but has yellow milk

Also known as the Mild Toadstool, this species is very common in oak woods, even on poor soils. It has a mild taste and, if cooked, is an edible species though it cannot be much recommended for culinary purposes. The slightly zoned, reddish-brown cap, streaky stem and unusual oily smell are distinctive.

RUSSULACEAE

Rufous Milk-cap
Lactarius rufus

ID FACT FILE

CAP: 4–8 cm, convex, expanding, with central boss, reddish-brown. Taste very hot. Milk white, unchanging

STEM: To 8 cm high, cap colour, paler at base

GILLS: Adnate-decurrent, paler than cap, crowded. Spores white

HABITAT: Pine woods, sometimes with birch

SEASON: Summer–autumn

LOOKALIKES: Curry-scented Milk-cap (p. 70) has a mild taste and a curry smell

A common and widespread species of pine woods, especially on acid soils, but in some areas also found with birch. It is a distinctive species, often fruiting in large numbers, and is easy to recognise by the rich rufous-brown cap with pointed central boss, and by its hot taste. The species has been used as a seasoning, but this is unwise and it is best avoided.

RUSSULACEAE

Woolly Milk-cap
Lactarius torminosus

J	F	M	A	M	J
J	A	S	O	N	D

ID FACT FILE

CAP: 6–12 cm across, convex, depressed and slightly slimy at centre, margin inrolled, woolly-hairy, pinkish with deeper-coloured concentric zones. Flesh white. Milk white, hot to taste

STEM: 5–8 cm high, 1–2 cm wide, finely downy, pale flesh colour, often with pinkish spots or pits

GILLS: Slightly decurrent, pinkish. Spores cream to yellowish

HABITAT: Woods, with birch

SEASON: Late summer–late autumn

LOOKALIKES:
L. mairei is more red-brown. *L. pubescens* has cap unzoned, whitish to cream. *L. cilicioides* has yellow milk

An attractive and generally common species. It is regarded as poisonous due to its very acrid taste, and has also been known by the common name of Griping Toadstool. It is, nevertheless, eaten in parts of Europe, especially after salting, but cannot be recommended. There are several similar species, but the woolly margin, colour and zonation of the cap and its association with birch are distinctive.

RUSSULACEAE

J	F	M	A	M	J
J	A	S	O	N	D

Ugly Milk-cap
Lactarius turpis

ID FACT FILE

Cap: 6–18 cm, dark olive-brown, zoned, slimy, depressed at centre, margin at first woolly, incurved. Milk white. Taste very hot

Stem: Short, stout, 3–6 × 2–3 cm, olive-brown

Gills: Crowded, cream with olive-brownish spots. Spores white

Habitat: Under birch, in woods and on heaths

Season: Late summer–late autumn

Lookalikes: *L. blennius* is usually smaller, with spotted cap

Highly distinctive on account of the large, rather slimy, dirty-olive cap, short stem and very hot taste. A drop of ammonia applied to any part of the fruitbody produces a violet reaction. It is a comparatively unattractive species, but the popular name nevertheless is a bit extreme. This is a common species in woods, also on heaths and in boggy places where birches grow.

PLUTEACEAE

Fawn Shield-cap
Pluteus cervinus

ID FACT FILE

CAP: 3–10 cm, convex to flattened, dark sooty brown becoming paler

STEM: Whitish, streaked with brown fibrils

GILLS: Free, crowded, at first white, becoming pink. Spores pink

HABITAT: Rotten wood, mostly of deciduous trees

SEASON: Mostly summer–autumn

LOOKALIKES: *P. salicinus* is more grey and has white stipe

Common in Europe on rotten logs and stumps. Usually solitary. The cap is very dark sooty brown at first and the gills are white. Known as the Fawn Shield-cap not for its colour, but because it is said to be eaten at times by deer; the alternative name Deer Mushroom is sometimes used. The species is edible, but is tasteless when cooked and not worthwhile.

PLUTEACEAE

Yellow Shield-cap

Pluteus chrysophaeus

ID FACT FILE

CAP: 1.5–4 cm across, at first conical, expanding, olive-yellow to yellow-brown, finely striate, more yellow when dry, sometimes veined at centre

STEM: 3–6 cm high, cylindric, pale cream, smooth, base white-hairy

GILLS: Free, crowded, yellowish-pink then pink. Spores pink

HABITAT: On rotten deciduous wood

SEASON: Autumn

LOOKALIKES: *P. leoninus* is bright golden yellow. *P. phlebophorus* has dark brown cap

An uncommon but rather attractive and distinctive species, growing alone or in groups on rotten deciduous logs. There are several yellowish species of *Pluteus*: in addition to those noted below, *P. romellii* is recognised by some authors, distinguished by its lemon-chrome stem and cap bay-brown with yellow margin. *Pluteus luteovirens*, used by some authors, is a synonym.

PLUTEACEAE

Veined Shield-cap

Pluteus umbrosus

ID FACT FILE

CAP: 4–10 cm, convex, brown, often ridged and veined, velvety, veins with darker, erect scales, margin fringed

STEM: 3–9 × 0.5–1 cm, often bulbous at base, whitish with fine velvety brown scales

GILLS: Free, whitish at first, soon pinkish with dark brown edge. Spores pink

HABITAT: On rotten wood of deciduous trees

SEASON: Autumn

LOOKALIKES: Highly distinctive and unlikely to be confused with other species

An attractive species which can be easily recognised by the conspicuous dark scales on its cap and the stem and the dark edge to the gills. It is not uncommon, occurring on rotten deciduous wood, especially that of elm, beech and ash, and is found throughout Europe. Edible when cooked, but poor and not recommended.

PLUTEACEAE

| J | F | M | A | M | J |
| J | A | S | O | N | D |

Silky Volvar
Volvariella bombycina

ID FACT FILE

Cap: 6–18 cm, bell-shaped, whitish or cream, covered with hair-like silky fibrils

Stem: 6–12 cm long, swollen at the base, arising from a sac-like volva. Volva white to brownish

Gills: Crowded, free, white then pink. Spores pink

Habitat: Decaying deciduous trees, especially elm

Season: Summer –autumn

Lookalikes: Unmistakable when in good condition

An attractive and easily recognised species, but rather rare. It occurs on various trees, but is most frequent on elm; indeed, it is one of several species which became commoner, in Britain at least, in the wake of Dutch Elm disease. It is now becoming rarer again. Considered a good edible species.

PLUTEACEAE

Slimy Volvar
Volvariella gloiocephala

ID FACT FILE

CAP: 5–10 cm, egg-shaped, expanding, whitish to grey-brown, slimy when wet

STEM: 6–9 cm high, white, arising from white or greyish volva

GILLS: Crowded, free, white then pink. Spores pink

HABITAT: Straw, compost, manure etc.

SEASON: Summer –autumn

LOOKALIKES: *Amanita* species may be similar, but have white gills and spores and usually a ring on the stem

Commonly known as *V. speciosa*, and popularly also as the Rose-gilled Grisette. It is quite common in appropriate places, and the largest of the European *Volvariella* species, distinguished as a genus by their pink spores and by the presence of a volva but no ring. The related Asian species, *V. volvacea*, the Padi Straw Mushroom, is an important edible species now cultivated in many areas.

ENTOLOMATACEAE

Roman Shield

Entoloma clypeatum

ID FACT FILE

CAP: 4–10 cm, bell-shaped, expanding, with central boss, smooth, dull yellow-brown to grey-brown, streaky, paler when dry. Mealy smell

STEM: 3–8 cm high, 1–2 cm thick, white to greyish, powdery at top

GILLS: Adnate, white to greyish, becoming pinkish with spores. Spores pink

HABITAT: Associated with rosaceous trees and shrubs

SEASON: Spring–early summer

LOOKALIKES: *E. aprile* is more slender and grows with elm

Fairly common, appearing in spring and early summer, and one of the few species of this genus which are safe to eat. It grows in mycorrhizal association with rosaceous trees and shrubs and, although it is a variable species, this together with its appearance in spring, the umbonate cap and pinkish gills make it fairly easy to recognise. It also has a strong, distinctive floury smell.

ENTOLOMATACEAE

| J | F | M | A | M | J |
| J | A | S | O | N | D |

Common Pink-gill
Entoloma rhodopolium

Widespread in Europe, and generally a common species of damp woodland, often growing in large groups. The white stem, grey-brown cap and lack of smell are characteristic, but there are many species of *Entoloma* and microscopic examination is necessary for positive determination of most species.

ID FACT FILE

CAP: 3–7 cm, convex to flattened, grey-brown, drying paler, smooth. Odour absent

STEM: 4–9 cm high, cylindric, whitish, slender

GILLS: Adnate to sinuate, whitish, then pink as spores mature. Spores pink

HABITAT: Deciduous woods

SEASON: Summer–autumn

LOOKALIKES: *E. nidorosum* is more brown and has distinct nitrous odour

ENTOLOMATACEAE

Silky Pink-gill

Entoloma sericeum

ID FACT FILE

Cap: 3–6 cm, convex then expanding, often with central boss, dark brown, silky, drying much paler. Smell mealy

Stem: 3–6 cm high, slender, greyish-brown with whitish base

Gills: Adnate or adnexed, rather crowded, soon becoming pink as spores mature. Spores pink

Habitat: Amongst grass, in fields, lawns etc.

Season: All year, mostly early summer–early winter

Lookalikes: *E. sericeoides*, in dry grassland, has cap strongly depressed

Common throughout most of Europe, occurring in damp, grassy places, often on lawns. The dark brown cap has a distinctive, silky shine when fresh, rapidly fading and paling as it dries. The length of the stem varies according to the length of grass in which the specimen is growing.

ENTOLOMATACEAE

| J | F | M | A | M | J |
| J | A | S | O | N | D |

The Miller
Clitopilus prunulus

ID FACT FILE

CAP: 4–10 cm, whitish, convex at first, later depressed, margin wavy. Taste and smell strong of flour

STEM: 2–4 × 1 cm, white, slightly tapered, lacking ring

GILLS: Decurrent, creamy becoming pinkish when mature. Spores pink

HABITAT: Deciduous woods

SEASON: Late summer–autumn

LOOKALIKES: Some species of *Clitocybe*, but these have white gills and spores

Common in open woods, and a good edible species. It has a strong odour of meal, from which the common name is derived. The cap surface is soft and matt rather like a kid glove, and this is a distinctive species. However, the noted lookalikes are poisonous and it must be gathered with care.

TRICHOLOMATACEAE

Tawny Funnel-cap
Lepista inversa

CAP: 4–9 cm, convex with centre indented then funnel-shaped, tawny-brown, smooth, margin incurved

STEM: To 5 cm high, cap colour, woolly at base

GILLS: Decurrent, whitish to cream, crowded. Spores pale cream

HABITAT: Coniferous and deciduous woods

SEASON: Autumn–early winter

LOOKALIKES: *Clitocybe infundibuliformis*, has wavy margin and pale tan cap

Often known as *Clitocybe flaccida*, this is a common woodland species. It is rather variable in colour, pale forms sometimes being distinguished as *L. gilva*. In its typical form, with tawny or orange-brown cap, circular in outline and becoming undulate only in old and large specimens, this is usually easy to recognise.

TRICHOLOMATACEAE

| J | F | M | A | M | J |
| J | A | S | O | N | D |

Wood Blewit

Lepista nuda

ID FACT FILE

Cap: 6–12 cm, convex, expanding, violaceous, fading to brown

Stem: Cap colour, swollen at base

Gills: Adnate, crowded, pale blue-violaceous. Spores pale pinkish

Habitat: Woods, parks, amongst leaf litter

Season: Late autumn–early winter

Lookalikes: Field Blewit (p.8) has pale cap and gills. Some *Cortinarius* species have brown spores, and may be poisonous

This species typically appears late in the season, and is often found after the first frosts. It is fairly common, growing in grass and amongst leaf litter in parks and woods, and even in gardens. It is a good edible species, much sought after, in fact, as there are few others available late in the season, but it should not be eaten uncooked.

TRICHOLOMATACEAE

J	F	M	A	M	J
J	A	S	O	N	D

Field Blewit

Lepista saeva

ID FACT FILE

Cap: 6–12 cm, convex to flattened or depressed, pale clay

Stem: Bluish-lilac, fibrillose

Gills: Adnate, crowded, cap colour. Spores pale pinkish

Habitat: Grassy places

Season: Autumn–early winter

Lookalikes: Wood Blewit (p.88) has violet cap and gills

Also known as Blue-leg, this is less common than Wood Blewit, and distinguished by the lack of violet colours in cap and gills. Like that species, it is also most often found rather late in the season. It occurs particularly in old grassland, and may form fairy rings. Like Wood Blewit it is a good edible species but must be well cooked first.

TRICHOLOMATACEAE

J	F	M	A	M	J
J	A	S	O	N	D

Netted Rhodotus
Rhodotus palmatus

An attractive and highly distinctive species which occurs mainly on decaying elm logs. In recent years it has become comparatively common in Britain in the wake of Dutch Elm disease. The cap cuticle is thick and gelatinous and wrinkles strongly as it dries. Inedible on account of its unpleasant, bitter taste.

ID FACT FILE

CAP: 4–10 cm, pinkish, with a network of raised wrinkles, gelatinous

STEM: Eccentric, short, to 5 cm long, 1–1.5 cm thick, pale pinkish

GILLS: Adnexed or adnate, distant, pinkish. Spores salmon-pink

HABITAT: On dead wood, usually of elm

SEASON: Autumn–early winter

LOOKALIKES: None

BOLBITIACEAE

Spring Field-cap
Agrocybe praecox

ID FACT FILE

CAP: 3–8 cm, convex, pale yellowish-brown, smooth or with cuticle cracking

STEM: 5–10 × 0.5–1 cm, whitish, with membranous ring, cylindric, base somewhat swollen

GILLS: Adnexed, crowded, at first whitish, becoming reddish-brown. Spores snuff-brown

HABITAT: Among grass, roadside verges, parks, open woods

SEASON: Mostly May–June

LOOKALIKES: Pale Field-cap (*A. dura*) is paler and has veil remains on cap edge

J	F	M	A	M	J
J	A	S	O	N	D

A frequent species, usually occurring in spring, but occasionally found later in the year. It is sometimes found singly, but often grows in groups. It is recognised by the colour, the ring on the stem and the rather floury smell, though there are several similar species. Said to be edible, but not recommended.

BOLBITIACEAE

Yellow Cow-pat Toadstool

Bolbitius vitellinus

J A S O N D

ID FACT FILE

CAP: 2–4 cm, conical to bell-shaped, bright yellow, brownish with age, sticky

STEM: Slender, fragile, hollow, whitish to pale yellow

GILLS: Free, thin, at first pale yellow, then brownish; spores brown

HABITAT: Rich soil, manure

SEASON: Early summer to late autumn

LOOKALIKES: None when in fresh condition

Common on rich soil and manure, often early in the season. The sticky yellow cap and thin, fragile flesh are characteristic. *Bolbitius titubans*, recognised by some authors, differs in being smaller and more delicate, and is uncommon. Another species, *B. reticulatus*, grows on wood and has a wrinkled, brownish cap. It is rather like a small *Pluteus* and was once placed in the genus *Pluteolus*.

BOLBITIACEAE

J	F	M	A	M	J
J	A	S	O	N	D

Milky Cone-cap
Conocybe lactea

ID FACT FILE

Cap: 1–1.5 cm across, 1–2 cm high, bell-shaped, scarcely expanding, whitish to cream, radially wrinkled, margin striate

Stem: 6–11 cm high, slender, with basal bulb, white, finely downy

Gills: Adnexed to free, crowded, pallid, becoming rusty with white edge. Spores ochre-brown

Habitat: Grassy places, parks, meadows

Season: Late summer–autumn

Lookalikes: None; the tall, pale cap and stem are distinctive

Quite common and widespread in various grassy places, including gardens, and also recorded from sand-dunes. A slender, fragile species which was once placed in the genus *Bolbitius*. The pale, whitish, rather slender conical cap is distinctive, and it can usually be readily recognised in the field, unlike many species of *Conocybe*.

CORTINARIACEAE

| J | F | M | A | M | J |
| A | S | O | N | D | |

Moss Pixy-cap

Galerina hypnorum

ID FACT FILE

CAP: 4–10 mm across, bell-shaped to hemi-spherical, orange-brown, paler when dry, striate almost to centre

STEM: To 3 cm high, slender, paler than cap, smooth

GILLS: Adnate, yellowish to rust-brown. Spores rust-brown

HABITAT: In moss in woods and on heaths, often in groups

SEASON: Summer –autumn

LOOKALIKES: Several other *Galerina* species appear similar and can be distinguished only on microscopic characters

The species occurs in various kinds of moss in woods or more open areas, growing singly or in groups. It is probably common, though confusion with other species has made its true distribution uncertain. Others, such as *G. cerina* and *G. calyptrata*, are very similar in appearance and habitat, and require microscopic examination for accurate identification.

CORTINARIACEAE

J	F	M	A	M	J
J	A	S	O	N	D

Autumn Pixy-cap
Galerina autumnalis

An extremely poisonous species, containing the same toxins as the Death Cap; indeed serious cases of poisoning by this and closely related species have been reported from both Europe and North America. It is fairly common, recognised by the ring, the almost smooth stem and habitat on rotten deciduous wood.

ID FACT FILE

CAP: 1.5–5 cm across, convex to flattened, striate, yellow-brown to tawny, paler when dry

STEM: 3–8 cm high, 3–5 mm thick, cap colour to yellowish-brown, ring present but often lost with age

GILLS: Adnate, rather crowded, pale brown then tawny to rust. Spores tawny-brown

HABITAT: On stumps and logs of deciduous trees

SEASON: Autumn

LOOKALIKES: *K. mutabilis* (p.96), also on deciduous trees, has scaly stem below the ring. *G. marginata* on conifers is very similar and equally poisonous

CORTINARIACEAE

Two-toned Wood-tuft
Kuehneromyces mutabilis

J F M A M J
J A S O N D

ID FACT FILE

CAP: 3–7 cm, convex or with central boss, orange-brown, drying pale ochraceous from the centre

STEM: To 8 cm high, with ring, dark brown scaly below ring, smooth and paler above

GILLS: Adnate, pale cinnamon. Spores ochre-brown

HABITAT: Stumps of deciduous trees

SEASON: Summer–autumn

LOOKALIKES: *G. marginata* on conifers and *G. autumnalis* (p.95) on deciduous wood lack scaly stem

Common, growing in tufts on rotten stumps of a variety of deciduous trees. The cap is distinctly hygrophanous, drying markedly paler from the centre outwards and forming a darker marginal zone, hence the popular name. This is a good edible species, but must not be confused with the highly toxic Autumn Pixy-cap (p.95).

AGARICACEAE

Golden Cap
Phaeolepiota aurea

| J | F | M | A | M | J |
| J | A | S | O | N | D |

ID FACT FILE

CAP: 8–15 cm across, convex, bright yellow-brown, minutely scaly

STEM: 10–18 cm high, with ring large and sprea-ding, marked underneath with ridge-like rows of granular scales

GILLS: Adnate, crowded, whitish then yellowish to ochraceous. Spores brown

HABITAT: Parks, woods

SEASON: Late summer–late autumn

LOOKALIKES: *Rozites caperata* has been con-fused with it but lacks mealy sur-face and large ring

A large and attractive species, highly distinctive on account of the bright golden-yellow colour and ring characters. It is frequent in much of Europe though erratic in its appearance. Often considered to be edible, though some cases of possible poisoning by this species have been reported from N America and it is probably best avoided.

STROPHARIACEAE

Charcoal Scale-head
Pholiota highlandensis

ID FACT FILE

Cap: 2–5 cm across, ochre-brown, slimy, convex to flattened; margin with veil remains. Flesh pale yellow

Stem: 3–7 cm high, with ring zone, yellow-brown, darker to base

Gills: Adnate, crowded, clay-brown. Spores brown

Habitat: Burnt ground

Season: Summer–autumn

Lookalikes:
P. spumosa is brighter yellow, more slimy and grows under conifers

Previously known as *P. carbonaria* from its habitat on burnt ground. Fairly common, sometimes solitary but usually growing in clusters. The species was once placed in *Flammula*, now recognised only as a subgenus of *Pholiota*, used for species with bright colours and a ring zone.

STROPHARIACEAE

J	F	M	A	M	J
J	A	S	O	N	D

Shaggy Scale-head
Pholiota squarrosa

ID FACT FILE

CAP: 4–11 cm, convex, expanding, tawny-yellow, dry, densely covered with recurved russet-brown scales

STEM: To 15 cm high, scaly below ring, tapered at base, cap colour

GILLS: Adnate, crowded, pale yellowish, then rusty. Spores brown

HABITAT: In clumps at base of trees

SEASON: Late summer–late autumn

LOOKALIKES: *P. squarrosoides* has somewhat greasy cap and smaller spores; *P. aurivella* has sticky cap with adpressed scales and grows high up on trees

A large and distinctive species which grows in clumps, usually at the base of deciduous trees, especially beech and ash. It is a weak parasite, entering the tree through wounds. Recognised by the habit and the dry, densely scaly cap and stem. Slightly poisonous, often causing digestive upsets.

CORTINARIACEAE

Red-banded Web-cap
Cortinarius armillatus

ID FACT FILE

CAP: 6–12 cm, convex to flat, brick to rusty-brown, dry, fibrillose. Odour radish-like

STEM: Tall, pale, with 3 or 4 oblique reddish bands, swollen below

GILLS: Adnate, whitish then rusty brown. Spores brown

HABITAT: Mainly with birch, on acid soil

SEASON: Late summer–autumn

LOOKALIKES: *C. veregregius*, with pinkish zones on stem

A well-known, large and distinctive species, one of the comparatively few of this genus which can be recognised with confidence. The red bands on the stem are distinctive. Fairly common in Europe, usually growing in damp birch woodland, especially on acid soils.

CORTINARIACEAE

Pelargonium Web-cap
Cortinarius paleaceus

A small, fairly common species, distinctive in its sharply conical cap, marked odour of *Pelargonium* and violaceous colour at the stem base. The fine hair-like scales on the cap are also characteristic, although similar hairs occur also in a few other related species.

ID FACT FILE

CAP: 1–3 cm, bell-shaped with acute central boss, dark brown covered with fine whitish scales. Drying paler. Distinct odour of *Pelargonium*

STEM: 5–8 cm high, brownish, with violaceous tinge at base and bands of whitish scales

GILLS: Adnate, lilac then cinnamon, crowded. Spores red-brown

HABITAT: Damp ground in deciduous woods

SEASON: Autumn

LOOKALIKES: *C. paleiferus* lacks violet at stem base; *C. hemitrichus* is larger and lacks odour and violet tint

J F M A M J J A S O N D

CORTINARIACEAE

Shining Web-cap
Cortinarius elatior

ID FACT FILE

CAP: 4–9 cm, conical, expanding, yellow-brown, often with violet tint at margin, radially wrinkled, sticky, shiny when dry

STEM: Slimy, tapered below cortina, white above, covered with violaceous slime below

GILLS: Adnate, pale violaceous then rust-brown with lilac edge. Spores rust-brown

HABITAT: Woods, especially with beech and mainly on clay soil

SEASON: Late summer to autumn

LOOKALIKES: *C. pseudosalor* has violaceous colour in stem

A fairly common fungus belonging to sub-genus *Myxacium*, comprising mostly large species in which both the cap and stem are slimy. The slimy stem is characteristic of *C. elatior*, separating the species from the similar and also fairly common *C. pseudosalor* that has violaceous colour in stem. According to some authors it is the same as *C. stillatitius*, but that occurs in coniferous forests.

CORTINARIACEAE

| J | F | M | A | M | J |
| J | A | S | O | N | D |

Purplish Web-cap
Cortinarius purpurascens

ID FACT FILE

Cap: 8–15 cm, convex, bay-brown, with violet tint at margin. Flesh blue-violet

Stem: Stout, blue-violaceous, bulbous at base

Gills: Sinuate, deep violet then rust brown, bruising violet. Spores rust-brown

Habitat: Mixed woods

Season: Autumn

Lookalikes: *C. caesiocyaneus*, blue-violet throughout, occurs on chalky soil with beech

A large and distinctive species, a member of the sub-genus *Phlegmacium* which includes large species in which the cap is slimy but the stem is dry. Frequent, occurring with both deciduous trees and conifers and distinguished from similar species by the blue-violet bruising of gills and stem. Although edible, it is best avoided because of possible confusion with other, poisonous species.

CORTINARIACEAE

Blood-red Web-cap
Cortinarius sanguineus

ID FACT FILE

Cap: 2–4 cm, convex to flattened, dry, slightly felty-scaly, blood red to carmine

Stem: 5–9 cm high, slender, cap colour, base paler

Gills: Adnate, blood red, rather crowded. Spores rusty-brown

Habitat: Coniferous woods

Season: Autumn

Lookalikes:
C. cinnabarinus is less slender and occurs in beech woods. *C. anthracinus*, with conifers, is a more brownish red

A typical member of subgenus *Dermocybe*, which includes species with dry cap and stem and usually brightly coloured, red to orange or tawny. These colours can be extracted by boiling and are excellent for dyeing wool. Species of *Dermocybe* may be similar and difficult to identify with certainty, but the bright red colour of *C. sanguineus* is characteristic. It is occasional to frequent in coniferous woods throughout Europe.

CORTINARIACEAE

Foxy Orange Web-cap
Cortinarius speciosissimus

J	F	M	A	M	J
J	A	S	O	N	D

ID FACT FILE

CAP: 5–9 cm, broadly conical, tawny or orange-brown, dry, felty

STEM: Cap colour, dry

GILLS: Adnate, tawny, distant. Spores rusty-brown

SEASON: Autumn

HABITAT: Under conifers, on acid soils

LOOKALIKES: *C. orellanus* and *C. orellanoides* occur under deciduous trees and are usually less conical. Both also deadly poisonous

A comparatively rare species, of northern distribution in Britain. This and some related species, notably *C. orellanus* and *C. orellanoides*, are deadly poisonous, containing the alkaloid, orellanin, which remains unaffected by cooking and drying. Symptoms do not appear for at least 36 hours after ingestion and last for several days, eventually leading to kidney failure after 7–17 days.

CORTINARIACEAE

| J | F | M | A | M | J |
| J | A | S | O | N | D |

Giant Flame-cap
Gymnopilus junonius

ID FACT FILE

CAP: 5–15 cm, convex, streaky or slightly scaly, bright rusty-orange

STEM: 8–18 cm long, with yellowish, spreading ring, stout, swollen to 2–3 cm thick towards the base then tapered

GILLS: Adnate, crowded, yellow to rusty. Spores brown

HABITAT: At base of deciduous trees, in tufts

SEASON: Late summer–late autumn

LOOKALIKES: *Pholiota squarrosa* is paler and has conspicuous, recurved scales

A large, impressive species which grows in tufts at the base of deciduous trees. It is the only member of the genus to have a ring on the stem and this, together with the bright rusty colours and distinctive stem shape, make it a comparatively easy species to identify. Inedible due to its bitter taste and presence of psilocybin.

CORTINARIACEAE

| J | F | M | A | M | J |
| J | A | S | O | N | D |

Freckled Flame-cap
Gymnopilus penetrans

ID FACT FILE

Cap: 2–7 cm, convex to flattened, bright rusty-tawny, slightly fibrillose

Stem: 3–6 cm high, 4–7 mm thick, yellow, fibrous

Gills: Adnate, yellowish to tawny, soon rusty spotted, crowded. Spores yellow-brown

Habitat: On branches and wood, especially in pine woods

Season: Late summer–late autumn

Lookalikes: *G. sapineus* is more scaly and restricted to conifers

Found throughout Europe, and generally a common species, sometimes fruiting in abundance. It is readily recognised by the rusty colours and spotted gills. Specimens with a veil leaving an indistinct ring-zone on the stem are sometimes separated as a distinct species, *G. hybridus*.

CORTINARIACEAE

| J | F | M | A | M | J |
| J | A | S | O | N | D |

Weeping Fairy-cake
Hebeloma crustuliniforme

ID FACT FILE

CAP: Convex,
4–8 cm, pale
clay-brown, cen-
tre darker, sticky.
Radish-like odour

STEM: 4–6 cm
high, whitish,
slightly swollen
at base, powdery
above. Veil
absent

GILLS: Clay-brown,
weeping small
droplets in wet
weather. Spores
brown

HABITAT: Deci-
duous woodlands

SEASON: Autumn

LOOKALIKES:
H. longicaudum
is paler and with
taller stem

A common toadstool of deciduous woods
throughout most of Europe. Sometimes known
as Poison Pie, it is toxic, causing severe
stomach cramps and diarrhoea. As with several
species of *Hebeloma*, this weeps droplets from
the gills in damp conditions. These form dark
brown spots when dry.

CORTINARIACEAE

Common Veiled Fairy-cake

Hebeloma mesophaeum

The commonest of those *Hebeloma* species which have a veil. This is usually quite easily seen forming a web-like covering towards the edge of the cap in mature fruitbodies. The species can be found in various habitats, in woods and on heaths, often on sandy soil, and occurs even in mountainous regions.

ID FACT FILE

CAP: 2–5 cm, convex to flattened, sticky, pale clay-brown, reddish-brown at centre, with web-like veil remnants at margin

STEM: 4–7 cm high, whitish, brownish below, with ring zone when young

GILLS: Sinuate, pale, becoming dull brown, crowded, not weeping. Spores pale brown

HABITAT: Woodlands, with conifers and birch, sometimes on burnt ground

SEASON: Late summer–late autumn

LOOKALIKES: *H. strophosum* has cap uniformly coloured, ring more conspicuous

CORTINARIACEAE

Straw-coloured Fibre-cap

Inocybe rimosa

ID FACT FILE

CAP: 2–7 cm, conical, expanding, with prominent centre, radially splitting, fibrous, straw-yellow. Mealy odour

STEM: 3–8 cm high, whitish or pale brown, lacking bulb

GILLS: Adnate, crowded, pale yellowish then clay-brown with white edge. Spores brown

HABITAT: Deciduous and coniferous woods

SEASON: Early summer–late autumn

LOOKALIKES: *I. arenicola*, in sand-dunes; *I. squamata* has less prominent umbo and cap less fibrous

Previously known as *I. fastigiata*, this is a common woodland species, occurring with various trees but especially favouring beech. Somewhat variable in form, but the conical, fibrous cap makes it fairly distinctive. Like many members of this genus, the species contains muscarine and can cause severe poisoning.

CORTINARIACEAE

Common White Fibre-cap
Inocybe geophylla

J	F	M	A	M	J
J	A	S	O	N	D

ID FACT FILE

Cap: 1.5–3 cm, conical, expanding, with prominent boss, silky, white, often yellowish at centre

Stem: To 6 cm high, white, cylindric, fibrous

Gills: Adnexed, creamy then clay brown. Spores snuff-brown

Habitat: Woodlands, path edges

Season: Summer –autumn

Lookalikes: *Entoloma sericella*, which differs in pink gills

One of the most common species of *Inocybe*, often growing in groups in woods, and found with both deciduous and coniferous trees. A lilac or violet form, var. *lilacina*, is also common, sometimes growing with the typical form. Both are poisonous, containing, as do many species of *Inocybe*, the sweat-inducing alkaloid muscarine.

CORTINARIACEAE

Common Veiled Fibre-cap

Inocybe maculata

ID FACT FILE

Cap: 2–7 cm, broadly conical, radially fibrillose, fawn-brown, usually with white veil remains at centre. Smell strong

Stem: 3–8 cm high, whitish then cap colour at centre, base rather bulbous

Gills: Adnate, pale grey-brown, edge white. Spores snuff-brown

Habitat: Woodlands, especially with beech

Season: Autumn

Lookalikes: *I. flavella* has smoother cap and lacks smell

Common and widespread in Europe, this is a woodland species which can often be found along path edges; it is most frequently found in beech woods on chalky soil. The whitish veil patches at the cap centre are usually distinct but may be absent in some specimens or lost with age.

CREPIDOTACEAE

Variable Slipper Toadstool

Crepidotus variabilis

ID FACT FILE

CAP: 0.5–2 cm across, fan-shaped, white, felty, laterally attached to substrate

STEM: Lacking

GILLS: Radiating from a point towards one side, whitish becoming pinkish-brown. Spores pale pinkish-brown

HABITAT: On dead stems and branches; common

SEASON: All year

LOOKALIKES: Several other species of *Crepidotus*, separated only on microscopic characters

Common and widely distributed, occurring usually on sticks and branches, but occasionally on herbaceous stems and other substrates. It is one of several common species of the genus which may occur in similar habitats and can be recognised with certainty only by microscopic examination.

CREPIDOTACEAE

Common Brownie

Tubaria furfuracea

ID FACT FILE

CAP: 2–3.5 cm, convex then flat, reddish-brown, drying paler, margin striate and with whitish scale-like patches of veil

STEM: 2–5 cm high, slender, slightly thicker at base, brownish

GILLS: Slightly decurrent, brown, rather distant. Spores yellowish-brown

HABITAT: Woods, waste ground, etc., often attached to wood

SEASON: All year, most frequent in autumn

LOOKALIKES: *T. conspersa*, less striate, covered with thin veil, gills less decurrent

A common species, usually growing solitary or in small groups, the fruitbodies commonly arising from fragments of wood. There are several related species, which require microscopic examination for positive identification. However, the striate cap and whitish, scale-like veil remnants usually present near the cap margin, and occasionally also forming a fibrous ring on the stem, are fairly distinctive.

AGARICACEAE

Horse Mushroom
Agaricus arvensis

J	F	M	A	M	J
J	A	S	O	N	D

ID FACT FILE

CAP: 10–15 cm, convex, whitish bruising yellowish, scales lacking

STEM: Up to 12 × 2.5 cm, white, cylindric, slightly thicker at base. Ring spreading, with cogwheel of soft, brownish scales beneath

GILLS: Whitish at first, dark chocolate-brown at maturity, crowded, free. Spores dark brown

HABITAT: Meadows, parks, in grassy places

SEASON: Late summer–autumn

LOOKALIKES: Yellow Stainer (p.120)

This is a good, edible species with a pleasant smell. It is fairly common, especially in fields and meadows in autumn, sometimes growing in fairy rings. The large, domed, white cap is characteristic, as is the yellowing of the surface with age or on bruising. It must not be confused with the poisonous Yellow Stainer (p.120) which smells unpleasant and also differs in having the stem base bright yellow when cut.

AGARICACEAE

The Prince
Agaricus augustus

ID FACT FILE

CAP: 10–25 cm, convex, expanding, with tawny-yellow scales. Bruises yellow; smell aniseed-like

STEM: 10–20 × 2–3 cm, whitish above, scaly below the large spreading ring

GILLS: At first pale pinkish-grey, becoming dark brown. Spores dark brown

HABITAT: Parks, open woods, usually under broadleaved trees

SEASON: Late summer–autumn

LOOKALIKES: Other scaly species, but these have cap and flesh bruising red

A large, attractive species which well deserves its common name. It is one of the few brown-scaly species of *Agaricus* in which the cap and stem stain yellowish on bruising; most others stain reddish. This, together with the pleasant aniseed-like smell, make it readily identifiable. Widespread and fairly common in Europe, and an excellent edible species.

AGARICACEAE

Pavement Mushroom

Agaricus bitorquis

ID FACT FILE

Cap: 5–10 cm, fleshy, convex to flattened, whitish, not scaly

Stem: 6–9 × 2–3 cm, whitish, with two rings

Gills: Pinkish at first, becoming dull red-brown. Spores dark brown

Habitat: Road-sides, pave-ments, wasteland

Season: Summer –autumn

Lookalikes: Other *Agaricus* species have a simple ring

The popular name of this species is quite apt; it is well known for its habit of pushing up paving stones, providing a good example of the power generated by growing hyphae. It is a good edible species, recognised by the presence of two rings on the stem, the lower one sheathing the stem base rather like a volva. Take care not to confuse it with poisonous *Amanita* species.

AGARICACEAE

Field Mushroom
Agaricus campestris

This is the true 'mushroom', a well-known and sought-after edible species, and one of the few that can safely be eaten raw. It occurs throughout temperate regions and can be found quite commonly in fields and meadows, sometimes forming fairy rings. However, it may grow amongst other species, so care is needed when collecting specimens for eating. It is also somewhat variable in colour and scaliness of cap.

| J | F | M | A | M | J |
| J | A | S | O | N | D |

ID FACT FILE

CAP: 4–10 cm, whitish to pale brown, smooth or slightly scaly. Flesh turns slowly pinkish when cut

STEM: Whitish, ring thin and often lost

GILLS: Free, pink, becoming reddish and finally dark brown. Spores dark brown

HABITAT: Fields, pastures

SEASON: Summer–autumn

LOOKALIKES: Yellow Stainer (p.120) is bright yellow in stem base. *Clitocybe* spp. (pp.30–2) have whitish, decurrent gills

AGARICACEAE

Scaly Wood Mushroom

Agaricus silvaticus

ID FACT FILE

Cap: 5–10 cm, becoming flat, pale brown with darker brown fibrous scales. Reddens when bruised

Stem: Whitish, slender, bulbous at base, with brownish ring

Gills: Free, at first whitish, soon pinkish, finally dark brown. Spores dark brown

Habitat: Coniferous woods

Season: Late summer–late autumn

Lookalikes: *A. haemorrhoidarius*, in deciduous woods. *A. langei* lacks bulbous stem base

One of the scaly woodland mushrooms with flesh which, at least in young, fresh specimens, becomes bright pinkish-red when cut or bruised. It is an excellent edible species with a pleasant smell. Common, usually amongst needle litter in conifer woods, and found throughout Europe. There are several other similar species, but these are also edible when cooked.

AGARICACEAE

Yellow Stainer
Agaricus xanthoderma

ID FACT FILE

Cap: 6–12 cm, convex, white or grey-brown, staining yellow on bruising. Unpleasant odour

Stem: Whitish, usually swollen at base, bright yellow in extreme base when cut, ring large, scaly below

Gills: Pale, becoming pinkish and finally dark brown. Spores dark brown

Habitat: Gardens, parks, grassy areas, woodland edge

Season: Summer –late autumn

Lookalikes: Horse Mushroom (p.115) also yellows, but has pleasant smell and flesh in stem base not yellow

A poisonous species to most people, sometimes causing alarming symptoms. Often very similar to edible mushrooms, especially Horse Mushroom (p.115) but recognised by its unpleasant, inky smell – which is more pronounced on cooking – and by the bright yellow flesh in the stem base. Some forms are greyish, with scaly cap. The closely related *A. praeclaresquamosus* has cap covered with small, sooty-brown scales, and is also poisonous.

COPRINACEAE

Common Ink-cap
Coprinus atramentarius

One of the most common of the ink-caps, usually growing in large tufts, and often found in man-made habitats, sometimes even pushing up through asphalted surfaces. It was once actually used for making ink, by boiling the mature, blackening caps. This species is edible, but must never be consumed with alcohol when it causes nausea, sweating and palpitations – symptoms identical to those of antabuse used in the treatment of alcoholism.

ID FACT FILE

CAP: 3–6 cm across, 3–7 cm high, oval or bell-shaped, expanding, greyish-white or pale fawn, slightly scaly at centre

STEM: Whitish, fragile, slightly thicker downwards, then rooting below ridge-like ring-zone

GILLS: Narrow, free, greyish, becoming black and deliquescing as the spores develop. Spores blackish-brown

HABITAT: On soil in woods and parks, growing from buried wood

SEASON: Early summer–late autumn

LOOKALIKES: *C. acuminatus* has narrower, more pointed cap and narrower spores, uncommon in woods

COPRINACEAE

Shaggy Ink-cap
Coprinus comatus

ID FACT FILE

CAP: 5–12 cm high, cylindric then narrowly conical, whitish, shaggy, brownish at the top. Flesh thin

STEM: Tall, hollow, white, with thin, loose ring below, and rooting base

GILLS: Ascending, free, white at first, soon pinkish from the base, blackening and deliquescing. Spores blackish

HABITAT: In grass, lawns, roadside verges etc.

SEASON: Summer–late autumn

LOOKALIKES: Unlikely to be confused with other species when in good condition. *C. sterquilinus* is smaller and on dung

Also known as Lawyer's Wig, this is a very common species, found in all kinds of grassy areas, roadsides and gardens. Readily recognised by the shaggy, narrowly conical cap which soon blackens from below and deliquesces into an inky fluid. It is a good edible species when young, while the gills remain white, but must be eaten very soon after gathering.

COPRINACEAE

| J | F | M | A | M | J |
| J | A | S | O | N | D |

Trooping Crumble-cap
Coprinus disseminatus

ID FACT FILE

CAP: 0.5–1.5 cm, bell-shaped, striate, finely hairy, greyish to pale fawn. Flesh very thin

STEM: Thin, to 3 cm high, pale grey, finely hairy

GILLS: Greyish, darker when mature. Spores blackish-brown

HABITAT: On and around stumps, and from buried wood

SEASON: Early summer–late autumn

LOOKALIKES: *Psathyrella pygmaea*, distinguished reliably only on microscopic characters

A common species, particularly in the south. Grows in dense clusters in various shady places, usually around old stumps or logs, and can be easily recognised by the habit, colour and small size. The fruitbodies are very delicate and rarely persist for more than about 24 hours. They may grow mixed with the superficially similar *Psathyrella pygmaea*. Too small and fragile to have any culinary interest.

COPRINACEAE

Glistening Ink-cap
Coprinus micaceus

ID FACT FILE

CAP: 2–4 cm across, bell-shaped or bluntly conical, expanding, grooved, pale orange-brown, covered with tiny mica-like particles

STEM: Whitish, fragile, hollow, variable in length

GILLS: Whitish at first, soon brown and finally blackish. Spores blackish-brown

HABITAT: Woodlands, parks, etc., usually around old stumps

SEASON: Spring–late autumn

LOOKALIKES: *C. truncorum* differs only in microscopic characters, but is rare

A common species, growing in large clusters on and around old stumps and logs of deciduous trees. Named for the shining, mica-like particles which cover the cap in young fruit-bodies; it has also been known as the Glittering Toadstool. Unlike some ink-caps, this shows only slight deliquescence and does not produce an inky fluid. It is generally regarded as an edible species, but cannot be recommended.

COPRINACEAE

Little Jap Umbrella
Coprinus plicatilis

ID FACT FILE

CAP: Cylindric, expanding to 1–2.5 cm across, strongly furrowed to smooth central zone, greyish-buff

STEM: Fragile, slender, to about 5 cm high, whitish

GILLS: Wide-spaced, greyish, attached to a collar around the stem. Spores purple-black

HABITAT: Parks, gardens, in grassy areas

SEASON: Late spring–autumn

LOOKALIKES: Several species, such as *C. galericuliformis* which occurs in woods, are distinguished by microscopic characters

A very common, delicate species which resembles a tiny umbrella owing to its strongly grooved cap. It is also known as the Plaited Toadstool. The fruitbodies are usually solitary, occasionally in small groups, and are thin-fleshed and ephemeral, soon curling up at the cap edge, and lasting only for a day. There are a number of similar species difficult to reliably distinguish without microscopic examination.

COPRINACEAE

J	F	M	A	M	J
J	A	S	O	N	D

Weeping Widow
Lacrymaria velutina

Aptly named for the droplets which weep freely from the gills in damp conditions. The species occurs throughout Europe and is fairly common, often growing in small clumps, especially on woodland paths. The black spores soon coat the woolly ring, and the species then has a distinctive appearance which makes it easy to recognise. Edible, but bitter to taste and not recommended.

ID FACT FILE

CAP: 4–10 cm, bell-shaped, with central boss, orange-brown, fibrillose becoming smooth, margin with white-woolly fringe

STEM: Whitish above, cap colour below, finely scaly below fibrous ring-zone

GILLS: Adnexed, crowded, soon dark brown with white edge, weeping droplets. Spores blackish

HABITAT: Parks, woodland paths, often in grass

SEASON: Early summer–late autumn

LOOKALIKES: *L. pyrotricha* is bright orange and much less common

COPRINACEAE

| J | F | M | A | M | J |
| J | A | S | O | N | D |

Hay-cap
Panaeolus foenisecii

ID FACT FILE

CAP: 1–2.5 cm across, convex, dark brown, drying paler from the centre

STEM: To 7 cm high, slender, fragile, paler than cap

GILLS: Adnate, pale brown soon mottled dark brown. Spores blackish-brown

HABITAT: Grassland

SEASON: Late spring–late autumn

LOOKALIKES: *P. subbalteatus* is larger and on manured or rich soil

Very common in grassy places, often on lawns, having a long fruiting period though most frequent in the autumn. It is also known as the Haymaker's Mushroom. The cap dries to a pale clay brown from the centre, leaving a characteristic dark brown margin. The species is said to be mildly hallucinogenic owing to the presence of indole compounds, but this is unproven.

COPRINACEAE

J	F	M	A	M	J
J	A	S	O	N	D

Shiny Hay-cap
Panaeolus semiovatus

ID FACT FILE

CAP: 2–5 cm across, ovate to bell-shaped, hardly expanding, pale clay to yellowish, smooth, sticky when damp

STEM: To 15 cm high, whitish, with thin ring, base bulbous

GILLS: Free, whitish then blackish-brown with white edge. Spores blackish

HABITAT: On horse and cattle dung

SEASON: Spring–late autumn

LOOKALIKES: *P. phalaenarum* lacks ring and has red tinges in cap and stem. *Stropharia semiglobata*, also with a ring, is smaller, less bell-shaped and has purple spores

One of the largest species on dung, widely distributed and often common. The ring on the stem is characteristic, but is thin and can be lost with age. Habitat and size and shape of cap, which is shiny when dry, should make it easy to recognise. Once referred to genus *Anellaria* on account of the ring on the stem.

COPRINACEAE

Fringed Hay-cap
Panaeolus sphinctrinus

ID FACT FILE

CAP: 2–3.5 cm across, bell-shaped, dark grey when fresh, drying pale, margin with fringe of whitish teeth

STEM: 5–12 cm high, slender, paler than cap

GILLS: Adnexed, blackish when mature, with white edge. Spores blackish

HABITAT: On dung in pastures

SEASON: Spring–autumn

LOOKALIKES: *P. campanulatus* is more brown and lacks distinct marginal teeth

Common, easily recognised by the whitish, dentate margin, which is formed from the remains of the veil. One of several dung-inhabiting *Panaeolus* species, and said to be mildly hallucinogenic, though the presence in this species of indole compounds (psilocin and psilocybin) which are responsible for such effects remains unproven.

COPRINACEAE

J	F	M	A	M	J
J	A	S	O	N	D

White Brittle-head
Psathyrella candolleana

ID FACT FILE

CAP: 2–5 cm, coni-cal or convex, pale yellow- brown to whitish, margin finely striate, often with scale-like remains of veil at margin, flesh brittle

STEM: 3–8 cm high, slender, hollow, white, smooth, fragile

GILLS: Adnexed, crowded, at first pinkish, then grey-brown to dark brown. Spores purple-brown

HABITAT: On roots and buried wood, often in clumps

SEASON: Summer–autumn

LOOKALIKES: None when typical

A common species, rather variable in colour and in development of the veil, but usually with a pale, almost whitish cap. This and its habit of growing in tufts from woody substrates should make it easy to recognise. However, as with all *Psathyrella* species microscopic examination is required to be certain of the identification.

COPRINACEAE

Rooting Brittle-head

Psathyrella gracilis

ID FACT FILE

Cap: 1–3 cm across, conical, scarcely expanding, striate at margin, dark brown to brown, drying paler with strong pink tinge

Stem: 3–10 cm high, slender, straight, whitish, base rooting and woolly

Gills: Adnate, grey-brown then purple-black, edge usually pinkish. Spores purple-black

Habitat: Woods, parks etc., often attached to dead wood

Season: Late summer–late autumn

Lookalikes: *P. microrhiza* has well-developed veil, and cap less pink on drying

A common woodland species, recognised by the rooting stem base and pink colours which develop on the cap when dry. In most specimens, the gill edge is also distinctly pinkish. It occurs singly or in small groups, usually in wooded habitats, often at path edges, and is found throughout Europe and in N America. This species is inedible.

COPRINACEAE

Common Stump Brittle-head

Psathyrella hydrophila

ID FACT FILE

Cap: 1.5–5 cm across, convex, expanding, red-brown to ochre-brown, drying paler, veil present forming fringe at margin

Stem: 3–7 cm high, white, hollow, brittle

Gills: Adnexed, crowded, pale brown then chocolate, edge white. Spores purple-brown

Habitat: In tufts on deciduous stumps

Season: Autumn–early winter

Lookalikes: *P. spadicea*, on stumps, lacks veil. *P. laevissima* is smaller and not in tufts. *P. fragrans* has fragrant odour and occurs on conifers

Widespread in Europe and often very common, particularly on beech and oak stumps. Amongst several similar but rarer species, noted below, it is recognised by the substrate, the well-developed veil and tufted habit. The white stem, which contrasts markedly with the cap and gill colour, is also characteristic.

COPRINACEAE

J	F	M	A	M	J
J	A	S	O	N	D

Scaly Brittle-head
Psathyrella artemisiae

ID FACT FILE

CAP: 2–3.5 cm across, conical or bell-shaped, remaining convex, red-brown, covered with thick, white cobwebby veil

STEM: 3–6 cm high, cylindric, whitish, hollow, fragile, white-downy

GILLS: Adnate, pale brown then dark grey-brown. Spores purple-black

HABITAT: On the ground in woods

SEASON: Summer–late autumn

LOOKALIKES: *P. pennata*, less common, occurs on burnt ground

A common species of both deciduous and coniferous woods, usually easily recognised due to the thick white veil which forms cottony scales on cap and stem, at least in fresh specimens. *Psathyrella pennata* is similar and also clothed in a thick, woolly veil, but grows on burnt ground.

STROPHARIACEAE

Peat Sulphur-cap
Hypholoma subericaeum

Occurs singly or in groups on damp, peaty soil, and is fairly common and widespread in Europe. The lack of yellow colours in the gills distinguishes it from the allied *H. ericaeoides*, but the very similar Heath Sulphur-cap *H. ericaeum* can be certainly differentiated only by its smaller spores.

ID FACT FILE

CAP: 2–5 cm, convex, often with low central boss, slightly greasy, smooth, fulvous, paler at the margin which often becomes striated with age. Margin may have distinct remains of the veil

STEM: 5–8 cm high, slender, 2–4 mm thick, whitish above, brownish below, hollow

GILLS: Adnate, rather crowded, pale, with olive tint then blackish with white edge. Spores purple-brown

HABITAT: On peaty soil on heaths and moors

SEASON: Autumn

LOOKALIKES: *H. ericaeoides*, in similar places, has yellow gills; *H. ericaeum* with smaller spores

STROPHARIACEAE

| J | F | M | A | M | J |
| J | A | S | O | N | D |

Sulphur Tuft
Hypholoma fasciculare

ID FACT FILE

Cap: 2–6 cm, pale sulphur yellow, bluntly conical, expanding, smooth, but often with scale-like remains of the veil at the margin

Stem: To 10 cm high, yellowish, tawny towards base, with slight ring-zone, trapping dark spores

Gills: Adnate, crowded, greenish-yellow, darkening as spores develop. Spores purple-brown

Habitat: Decaying stumps and logs

Season: Early summer–early winter

Lookalikes: *H. sublateritium* has brick-coloured cap and stem. *Pholiota alnicola* has brown spores

A common species which grows in dense tufts on rotten stumps and trunks of both deciduous and coniferous trees. The greenish gills of young fruitbodies are distinctive, as is the sulphur-yellow cap, though this is often covered eventually with a deposit of purple-brown spores from surrounding caps. The species is not poisonous but has a bitter taste and should not be eaten.

STROPHARIACEAE

J	F	M	A	M	J
J	A	S	O	N	D

Blueing Psilocybe
Psilocybe cyanescens

ID FACT FILE

CAP: 2–5 cm across, convex becoming flattened, slightly sticky, rusty-yellow drying paler, staining blue-green on handling and with age

STEM: 5–8 cm high, cylindric, with thin web-like veil, blue-green on handling

GILLS: Adnate, dark purple-brown, with whitish margin. Spores purple-brown

HABITAT: Wood chips, leaf litter, etc.

SEASON: Late summer–autumn

LOOKALIKES: None

Uncommon, but now spreading in S England. It was first described from Kew Gardens in 1946 and has since spread elsewhere in England and parts of Scotland, and is also present in other parts of Europe. Like many species with blueing flesh, this is mildly hallucinogenic due to the presence of psilocybin.

STROPHARIACEAE

J	F	M	A	M	J
J	A	S	O	N	D

Liberty-cap
Psilocybe semilanceata

ID FACT FILE

Cap: 5–20 mm across, bell-shaped to conical, with sharp central boss, not expanding, brown when fresh, drying yellowish-buff

Stem: 4–10 cm high, slender, paler than the cap, rarely bluish at base when handled

Gills: Adnate or adnexed, crowded, becoming purple-brown, with white edge. Spores purple-brown

Habitat: In grass, on lawns, fields, etc.

Season: Late summer–late autumn

Lookalikes: *P. strictipes* has cap broadly expanded with age

A well-known toadstool, widespread in Europe, and much sought after for 'recreational' purposes as it contains the hallucinatory drug psilocybin. It is common in most seasons in grassy areas, sometimes growing in large numbers. The pointed, bell-shaped cap, said to resemble the helmet of French soldiers, provides the inspiration for the common name and, with the slender stem, is characteristic.

STROPHARIACEAE

Orange Slime-cap
Stropharia aurantiaca

ID FACT FILE

Cap: 2–6 cm, convex, orange-red, slimy when moist

Stem: To about 10 cm high, whitish or with yellowish or orange tints below

Gills: Adnexed, whitish to yellowish. Spores dark purple-brown

Habitat: Clustered, mostly on wood-chip mulch in parks and gardens; coniferous and mixed woodland

Season: Autumn

Lookalikes: None

One of the most attractive of the slime-caps, this is an introduced species which has become frequent in some areas in recent years. It has spread particularly with wood chippings used as a mulch on flower beds, but also occurs occasionally in more natural habitats. Its orange-red cap, clustered habit and dark spores make it easy to recognise.

STROPHARIACEAE

J	F	M	A	M	J
J	A	S	O	N	D

Verdigris Toadstool

Stropharia aeruginosa

ID FACT FILE

Cap: 3–7 cm, convex or blunt-conical, blue-green fading to yellowish, slimy, with white-cottony veil scales especially near the margin. Flesh whitish

Stem: Cylindrical, 4–9 cm high, 5–9 mm thick, rather slimy, covered in white-cottony scales below the distinct ring

Gills: Adnate or slightly decurrent, pale greyish to violaceous-grey. Spores purple-brown

Habitat: Damp woodland

Season: Late summer–late autumn

Lookalikes: *S. cyanea*, common in damp grassy places, has a poorly developed ring

One of a group of closely related and attractive species with cap bright blue-green when fresh, but soon fading to yellowish. This attractive species, with a well-developed ring, is rather less common than some others of the group, but occurs in various kinds of woodland habitats, as well as in parks and grassy places. It is known to contain small quantities of psilocybin, and is likely to cause mild hallucinations if eaten.

BOLETACEAE

Cep
Boletus edulis

ID FACT FILE

CAP: 8–15 cm, hemispherical, often becoming flattened, brown, fleshy

STEM: 8–15 × 3–8 cm, stout, swollen below, whitish to buff, with distinct network of raised lines

PORES: Small, whitish to greenish-yellow, not staining when bruised. Spores yellow-olive

HABITAT: Coniferous and mixed woods

SEASON: Summer–autumn

LOOKALIKES: *B. aereus*, with oak, has dark brown cap and stem. *B reticulatus*, with beech, has stem netted to base. *B. pinophilus*, under pines, has dark brown cap

Also known as the Penny Bun. The most sought after of the boletes, this is an excellent edible species which can be dried for winter use. Of commercial importance, it is the species that is commonly used in mushroom soups. Sometimes common in coniferous woods, while closely related forms, such as those referred to as *B. aereus* and *B. reticulatus*, grow in deciduous forests.

BOLETACEAE

Dotted-stem Bolete
Boletus erythropus

ID FACT FILE

Cap: 6–15 cm across, convex to flattened, dark brown. Flesh yellowish, instantly bright blue when cut

Stem: Stout, to 5 cm thick, swollen below, dotted reddish throughout over yellow ground; bruising blue

Pores: Orange-red, bruising blue

Habitat: Deciduous and coniferous woods

Season: Summer–autumn

Lookalikes: *B. luridus* also turns blue but has network on stem

A fairly common and distinctive species, the red pores, red dotted stem and blueing flesh being diagnostic. It occurs in various wooded habitats on acid soils. The deep blue staining of the flesh on cutting is due to an oxidation reaction. Despite this, it is a good edible species but should be cooked before eating. However, note that some species with blueing flesh, including *B. luridus*, are mildly poisonous.

B. erythropus var. *immutatus*, a rare variety in which the flesh is unchanging when cut

BOLETACEAE

| J | F | M | A | M | J |
| J | A | S | O | N | D |

Devil's Bolete
Boletus satanas

A rare species confined to deciduous woods on calcareous soils. The whitish cap, red pores and netted stem are fairly distinctive, though several species, as noted below, may appear similar. This species, together with its close relatives, is mildly poisonous, a stomach irritant which may cause nausea and vomiting but does no serious harm.

ID FACT FILE

CAP: 10–25 cm, hemispherical, sometimes flattened, whitish to pale buff. Flesh slowly blueing when cut

STEM: Stout, to 10 cm thick, rather swollen below, reddish with yellow tints below, upper part with reddish network

PORES: Soon orange-red, blueing when bruised. Spores olive

HABITAT: On chalky soil, mostly with beech

SEASON: Summer–autumn

LOOKALIKES: *B. rhodoxanthus* has yellow-brown cap and stem netted to base. *B. splendidus* has grey-brown cap. *B. torosus* has yellow-brown cap and instantly blueing flesh

XEROCOMACEAE

Red-cracked Bolete
Xerocomus chrysenteron

ID FACT FILE

Cap: 5–10 cm, convex to flattened, brown, finely velvety, cracking to reveal reddish flesh

Stem: 5–7 × 1–1.5 cm, usually tapered, yellowish with red streaks

Pores: Angular, rather large, sulphur-yellow to greenish, bruising blue

Habitat: With trees, usually in woods

Season: Summer–autumn

Lookalikes: *X. subtomentosus*, *X. lanatus*, *X. pruinatus*, *X. armeniacus*, *X. rubellus*

One of the commonest of the boletes, easy to recognise in its typical form, with a reddish stem and distinct red layer below the cap cuticle, but a very variable species. Those noted under 'Lookalikes' may be very similar and require careful identification. All these species are usually placed in the genus *Xerocomus* because of their dry caps.

XEROCOMACEAE

| J | F | M | A | M | J |
| J | A | S | O | N | D |

ID FACT FILE

Cap: 4–12 cm, bay brown, convex, smooth. Flesh whitish, blue tinge on cutting

Stem: 4–10 × 0.8–2.5 cm, streaky, brownish, paler than cap

Tubes: Yellow, pores readily bruising blue-green

Habitat: Mixed woods

Season: Late summer–late autumn

Lookalikes: *B. spadiceus*, very rare, has network on stem

Bay Bolete
Xerocomus badius

Common in coniferous and sometimes deciduous woods, and a good edible species with firm flesh which has a pleasant nutty taste. It is somewhat variable in colour, but the streaky, brownish stem and blue-bruising pores are diagnostic. This species is sometimes placed in the genus *Boletus*.

BOLETACEAE

Bitter Bolete
Tylopilus felleus

ID FACT FILE

Cap: 5–12 cm, convex to flattened, some shade of brown. Flesh whitish, bitter

Stem: 8–12 cm high, thicker below, whitish then brownish, with distinct brownish network

Pores: White then pinkish; tubes pale pink. Spores pinkish-brown

Habitat: Coniferous and deciduous woods on acid soil

Season: Late summer–autumn

Lookalikes: Cep (p.140) has white net and olive-yellow pores

This is the only European species of a genus which is mainly American in distribution. It differs from other boletes mainly in its pinkish spores. *Tylopilus felleus* is fairly common and should be easy to recognise by the pinkish pore layer and conspicuous network-like pattern on the stem, although the cap colour is variable. The flesh has a markedly bitter taste, and the species is not edible, causing irritation of the digestive system even when cooked.

BOLETACEAE

| J | F | M | A | M | J |
| J | A | S | O | N | D |

Cow Bolete
Suillus bovinus

ID FACT FILE

CAP: 4–10 cm, convex, orange-buff to ochre-brown, slimy

STEM: 4–7 × 1–1.5 cm, cap colour, without glandular dots

PORES: Slightly decurrent, olive-brown, large, angular, subdivided. Tubes concolorous. Spores olive-brown

HABITAT: Pine woods on acid soil

SEASON: Late summer–late autumn

LOOKALIKES: *S. variegatus* has finely scaly cap and smaller pores. *S. flavidus* is brighter yellow and has a ring on the stem

The common name refers to the colour of the cap, said to resemble that of an Alderney cow. The flesh of the cap is thin and pale buff, usually turning slightly blue when cut. It grows under pines, usually *Pinus sylvestris*, in woods but also on heaths. This is an edible species, though poor and with little taste and cannot be recommended.

BOLETACEAE

| J | F | M | A | M | J |
| J | A | S | O | N | D |

Slippery Jack
Suillus luteus

ID FACT FILE

Cap: 5–10 cm, convex, very slimy, chestnut or purple-brown. Flesh pale yellowish, unchanging

Stem: 6–10 × 2–2.5 cm, apex pale yellowish with glandular dots, whitish with violet-brown tinge below large, white to purple-brown ring

Pores and tubes: Yellow. Spores ochre-brown

Habitat: Conifers, especially under pines

Season: Late summer–late autumn

Lookalikes: *S. grevillei*, with ring, has yellow cap and occurs with larch

Widespread and generally common in Europe, growing mostly with *Pinus sylvestris*. It is an edible species, sometimes also known as the Butter Bolete, but rather soft and not much recommended for such purposes. It is best dried after removing the slimy layer, which may cause digestive irritation to some people, and used as a flavouring.

BOLETACEAE

| J | F | M | A | M | J |
| J | A | S | O | N | D |

Brown Birch Bolete
Leccinum scabrum

ID FACT FILE

CAP: 5–12 cm, hemispherical, brown, smooth, soft. Flesh whitish, unchanging

STEM: 8–15 × 2–3 cm, cylindric, with grey, woolly scales on whitish ground

PORES: Whitish then dull grey-brown, small, unchanging when bruised. Spores brownish

HABITAT: In woods under birches

SEASON: Summer–autumn

LOOKALIKES: *L. carpini*, flesh turns reddish then violet-black. *L. duriusculum* is darker, flesh turns pinkish, under poplars. *L. holopus* with birch, but whitish throughout

A very common species, growing in mycorrhizal association with birch. It is edible, but not amongst the best because of its soft flesh. There are several closely related and similar species which may be difficult to distinguish, particularly when growing in mixed woods where the mycorrhizal partner is uncertain; the most frequent of these are noted below under 'Lookalikes'.

BOLETACEAE

Orange Birch Bolete
Leccinum versipelle

ID FACT FILE

Cap: 5–12 cm, hemispherical, orange-brown to brick-red

Stem: 8–15 × 2–3 cm, with blackish scales on whitish ground

Pores: Whitish then dingy grey, small. Spores brownish

Habitat: In woods under birch

Season: Summer–autumn

Lookalikes: *L. scabrum*, with birch, has brown cap and greyish stem scales. *L. aurantiacum* with aspen, and *L. quercinum*, with oak, have orange-brown stem scales

Grows in mycorrhizal association with birch and is a widespread species, still frequent but now less common in some areas than formerly. The orange cap and blackish stem scales are diagnostic. The flesh is white, but discolours vinaceous then blackish when cut, and sometimes blue-green in the stem base. This is a good edible species, having firm flesh with a mild, pleasant taste.

BOLETACEAE

| J | F | M | A | M | J |
| J | A | S | O | N | D |

Old Man of the Woods
Strobilomyces strobilaceus

A highly distinctive bolete owing to the coarse-ly scaly cap, but it is rare in Europe except in the south. Other similar species occur in the tropics and S hemisphere. This species is edi-ble, but, though regularly eaten in some areas and highly regarded by some, it is generally considered to have a rather bland, spongy flesh.

ID FACT FILE

CAP: 5–12 cm, convex, covered with thick scales, smoky-grey to blackish, margin often paler. Flesh whitish turning reddish

STEM: 6–10 × 1–2 cm, grey to grey-brown, soft-scaly, forming ring-zone in upper part

PORES: Large, white to greyish, bruising reddish. Spores violet-black

HABITAT: Mixed woods

SEASON: Summer–autumn

LOOKALIKES: None in Europe

GOMPHIDIACEAE

J	F	M	A	M	J
J	A	S	O	N	D

Pine Spike-cap
Chroogomphus rutilus

ID FACT FILE

CAP: 5–12 cm, convex, expanding, with central rather acute boss, ochrebrown with copper tints, slimy when wet

STEM: 6–10 cm high, 1–2 cm thick, cylindric, greyish-pink above, yellowish below, with slight ring-zone

GILLS: Decurrent, thick, widely spaced, olivaceous then blackish-brown. Spores olivebrown

HABITAT: Pine woods

SEASON: Late summer–autumn

LOOKALIKES: *C. helveticus* has dry, felty cap

A widespread and sometimes common species found in coniferous woodland growing solitary or in small groups. It is a distinctive species, recognised by the shape, the rather wine-coloured cap and the dark, rather waxy, strongly decurrent gills. It apparently occurs only with two-needled species of *Pinus*, such as *P. sylvestris*.

GOMPHIDIACEAE

Rosy Spike-cap
Gomphidius roseus

ID FACT FILE

Cap: 2–6 cm, convex to flattened or with central boss, reddish-pink, slimy

Stem: 3–6 cm high, tapered, whitish, base yellowish, slimy

Gills: Decurrent, distant, whitish then grey-black. Spores brown-black

Habitat: In pine woods, often with Cow Bolete (p.146)

Season: Late summer–autumn

Lookalikes: None

An attractive but uncommon species, readily distinguished by the reddish cap and white flesh. Occurs under pine on sandy, usually acid soils and, when seen from above, may resemble a species of *Russula*. It is often found in association with Cow Bolete (p.146), although the relationship between these species is unclear.

PAXILLACEAE

| J | F | M | A | M | J |
| J | A | S | O | N | D |

Velvet Roll-rim
Paxillus atrotomentosus

ID FACT FILE

CAP: 10–25 cm, brown, convex, centre depressed, margin inrolled

STEM: short, stout, to 8 × 5 cm, often eccentric, rooting, velvety, dark brown

GILLS: Decurrent, interconnected to form a network on the stem, crowded, cream. Spores ochrebrown

HABITAT: On stumps of conifers

SEASON: Late summer–autumn

LOOKALIKES: Brown Roll-rim (p.154) has slender, non-velvety stem

The stout, dark brown, velvety stem is the most characteristic feature of this species which is widespread and sometimes frequent in coniferous woods, particularly with pine. It is a saprophyte, growing on old stumps, and causing a brown rot. The species has a bitter taste and is probably poisonous.

PAXILLACEAE

Brown Roll-rim
Paxillus involutus

ID FACT FILE

CAP: Brown, convex then depressed at centre, sticky when damp, margin velvety, inrolled

STEM: 4–7 × 2–3 cm, cap colour

GILLS: Decurrent, yellow-brown, bruising purple-brown. Spores white

HABITAT: Woods, with birch

SEASON: Summer–autumn

LOOKALIKES: *P. rubicundulus* stains rust-brown and grows under alder

Aptly named because of the strongly inrolled cap margin, remaining so even in old specimens. The margin is at first rather woolly and has a characteristic 'scalloped' pattern of fine branching ridges. The gills bruise dark brown and can be easily removed from the cap, as can the tubes in boletes, to which *Paxillus* is closely related. A poisonous species, the toxin is cumulative causing potentially fatal haemolysis.

PAXILLACEAE

False Chanterelle
Hygrophoropsis aurantiacus

ID FACT FILE

Cap: 3–7 cm across, flat to depressed, orange-yellow, paling with age, dry and finely downy, margin inrolled

Stem: Tapered and often curved, 2–5 cm high, yellowish to orange-brown

Gills: Decurrent, crowded, forked, deep orange. Spores white

Habitat: In pine woods and on heaths

Season: Late summer–late autumn

Lookalikes: Chanterelle (p.159) has thicker gills and is egg-yellow

A common species in coniferous woodland and often mistaken for the true chanterelle which may grow in similar places. It differs especially in the thinner, crowded gills, and in colour. Although eaten by some people, this species may cause gastric upsets and is best avoided. A whitish form found in damp woods on acid soil is sometimes distinguished as a separate species, *H. pallida*.

whitish form *H. pallida* (below)

LENTINACEAE

Branched Oyster
Pleurotus cornucopiae

ID FACT FILE

CAP: 5–12 cm across, whitish to cream or pale yellowish, convex to depressed or funnel-shaped, margin often wavy

STEM: Central or slightly eccentric, tapered, often fused at the base, variable in length, with network formed by gills in upper part

GILLS: Strongly decurrent, rather distant, whitish, interconnected to a network below. Spores pale lilac

HABITAT: In clumps on rotten logs and stumps, especially of elm

SEASON: Late spring–autumn

LOOKALIKES: Other 'oyster' mushrooms on wood lack such decurrent gills and have eccentric stems

Fairly common, occurring mostly on elm, and having become particularly frequent in parts of Britain in the wake of Dutch Elm disease. Fruitbodies may appear, often in dense clusters, from spring until autumn, and are unlikely to be confused with other species; the deeply decurrent gills and central stem are distinctive and diagnostic. As are other species of *Pleurotus*, this is a good edible species.

LENTINACEAE

Oyster Mushroom

Pleurotus ostreatus

A well-known and sought-after edible fungus, increasingly grown commercially. The cap colour is very variable, and forms with strong blue tints (var. *columbinus*) are known, popularly called Peacock Fungus. Though perhaps most frequent on beech, it can occur on many trees, including conifers, and not uncommonly on worked timber. It causes a rapid decay, in the form of a white, flaky rot.

ID FACT FILE

CAP: 5–15 cm across, convex to flattened, greyish-brown, often with blue or lilac tints, fading, smooth or slightly scaly, margin wavy when old

STEM: Lateral or very eccentric, short, sometimes lacking, whitish, base woolly

GILLS: Decurrent, whitish. Spores pale lilac

HABITAT: In tiers on stumps and trunks of various trees

SEASON: All year, but mainly autumn

LOOKALIKES: *P. pulmonarius* is whitish and fruits mainly in late summer

TRICHOLOMATACEAE

J	F	M	A	M	J
J	A	S	O	N	D

Styptic Toadstool
Panellus stipticus

ID FACT FILE

CAP: 1–4 cm, kidney-shaped, with lateral stem, pale brown or fawn, scurfy

STEM: Very short, flattened, cap colour or often paler

GILLS: Crowded, cap colour, sometimes forked. Spores white

HABITAT: In tiers on stumps and dead branches, usually of oak

SEASON: Spring–early winter

LOOKALIKES: None

A common species, usually occurring as a saprophyte on dead wood, but rarely as a weak parasite, entering the host through wounds. It may also attack structural timber. In America, this species is said to have luminous gills, but this character is not known in European specimens. A distinctive species, recognized by the scurfy cap and short, rather flattened stem.

CANTHARELLACEAE

J	F	M	A	M	J
J	A	S	O	N	D

Chanterelle
Cantharellus cibarius

ID FACT FILE

CAP: 4–9 cm across, convex to flattened, soon depressed at centre, margin inrolled, wavy and often lobed, egg-yellow. Faint apricot-like odour

STEM: 4–7 cm high, tapered downwards, cap colour or paler, smooth, solid

GILLS: Deeply decurrent, rather thick, with blunt edges, shallow, vein-like, irregularly forked, cap colour. Spores ochraceous

HABITAT: Coniferous and deciduous woods, especially on sandy, acid soil

SEASON: Late summer–autumn

LOOKALIKES: *C. friesii* is smaller, in beech woods. False Chanterelle (p.155) is more orange on cap, with thin gills

This is one of the best edible fungi. It is much sought after and often seen for sale in Continental markets. It has an excellent flavour but is rather tough and should be cooked slowly. There is a white form of this species, and another, with reddish-purple scales, is known as var. *amethysteus*. The Chanterelle is seemingly less common now in many areas, perhaps due to pollution from acid rain.

CLAVARIADELPHACEAE

J	F	M	A	M	J
J	A	S	O	N	D

Giant Club
Clavariadelphus pistillaris

ID FACT FILE

FRUITBODY:
Simple, solitary
or in groups,
club-shaped,
rounded above,
yellowish-buff,
large, 8–20 ×
3–5 cm, some-
what wrinkled,
stalk not distinct.
Flesh whitish.
Spores ochra-
ceous

HABITAT: Woods,
especially with
beech

SEASON: Late
summer–autumn

LOOKALIKES:
C. truncatus has
a blunt top and
grows with
conifers. *C. ligula*
is smaller and
also grows with
conifers

A large and distinctive but rather rare fungus
found with beech trees on chalky soils. The
fruitbodies are rounded at the top, so that the
common name is quite apt. The related and
equally impressive *C. truncatus* has a markedly
flattened top and should be easy to distinguish.
The Giant Club is widespread in Europe, and
also known from N America.

CLAVARIACEAE

Heath Fairy-club
Clavaria argillacea

ID FACT FILE

FRUITBODY:
Simple, 3–6 cm high, 3–6 mm thick, club-shaped, blunt, pale yellowish, often with tinge of green. Stem distinct, slightly darker, fertile upper part often flattened and grooved. Spores white

HABITAT: On the ground on heath-land, moors, etc.

SEASON: Late summer–late autumn

LOOKALIKES:
C. straminea is straw-yellow and rare

Found throughout Europe and sometimes common on peaty ground, often growing on heaths or moors amongst heather. The simple, unbranched clubs, often growing in clusters, are sometimes found in abundance. They are pale yellow or with a greenish tinge, and this together with the habitat, should make the species easy to identify.

CLAVARIACEAE

J	F	M	A	M	J
J	A	S	O	N	D

Yellow Fairy-club
Clavulinopsis helvola

ID FACT FILE

FRUITBODY:
3–8 cm high,
yellow-orange,
simple,
unbranched,
usually rather
flattened, tip
blunt, stem
not distinct.
Spores white or
yellowish

HABITAT: In grass,
in lawns, parks,
etc.

SEASON: Late
summer–autumn

LOOKALIKES:
C. luteoalba is
apricot-yellow
and smaller. *C.
pulchra* is deeper
orange. Both
differ in spore
characters

One of the most common of the fairy-clubs,
growing in small clusters in various grassy
areas. In the field it may be confused with
other yellowish species, several of which are
found in similar habitats. It can be readily
identified under the microscope by its coarsely
warted spores, a rare character in such fungi.

CLAVULINACEAE

Crested Coral-fungus
Clavulina cristata

J	F	M	A	M	J
J	A	S	O	N	D

ID FACT FILE

FRUITBODY:
2.5–6 cm high,
whitish, much
branched, with
fine, acute tips.
Stalk stout,
short. Spores
white

HABITAT: Damp
ground in woods,
often in leaf litter

SEASON: Late
summer–late
autumn

LOOKALIKES:
C. cinerea, more
grey and less
finely branched

One of the most common of the fairy-club fungi, though sometimes hidden under leaf litter or other vegetation and easy to overlook. Somewhat variable in appearance, but the finely divided, pointed tips are distinctive. The species is sometimes attacked by a parasitic fungus, and then appears dark grey.

RAMARIACEAE

| J | F | M | A | M | J |
| J | A | S | O | N | D |

Straight Coral-fungus
Ramaria stricta

ID FACT FILE

FRUITBODY:
4–10 cm high, upright, much branched from the base, branches erect, straight, forked, pale buff often with pinkish tinge, tips yellowish. Stem usually distinct, short, thick, with whitish, root-like strands at the base. Flesh pale yellow-buff. Spores yellowish

HABITAT: On or around rotten wood

SEASON: Late summer–late autumn

LOOKALIKES: Other *Ramaria* species differ in colour and grow on soil

True Coral-fungi, species of *Ramaria*, are usually much-branched, and are distinguished from other groups by their yellowish spore-deposit. *Ramaria* is a large genus, the species often very difficult to identify. Many are now very rare. That included here is fairly common in woods and distinguished by its straight, erect branches and growth on wood.

SPARASSIDACEAE

Cauliflower Fungus
Sparassis crispa

J	F	M	A	M	J
J	A	S	O	N	D

ID FACT FILE

FRUITBODY:
20–35 cm across, cauliflower-like in form, with rooting base, cream to pale buff, sometimes brownish at lobe margins when old, densely branched, the branches flattened, lobed, wavy, brittle. Spores pale ochraceous

HABITAT: At the base of stumps and trunks of pines

SEASON: Summer–autumn

LOOKALIKES: *S. laminosa*, mostly with deciduous trees, has flattened, less crowded branches and is comparatively rare

Common in Britain, but rare in parts of Europe. This species grows from the roots of pine, and is parasitic, causing a slow rot of the heart wood at the base of the tree. It is a good edible fungus, and easy to recognise, but the fruitbodies should be carefully cleaned to remove dirt and grit from between the densely packed branches.

HYDNACEAE

| J | F | M | A | M | J |
| A | S | O | N | D | |

Hedgehog Fungus
Hydnum repandum

ID FACT FILE

Cap: 4–10 cm across, convex or depressed at centre, smooth, cream to pale buff or pinkish-buff

Stem: Short, to 7 cm high, sometimes eccentric, cap colour

Spines: Cap colour, 2–5 mm long, decurrent. Spores white

Habitat: In mixed woods

Season: Late summer–autumn

Lookalikes: *H. rufescens* has orange-brown cap and is more slender

Fairly common and widespread in Europe, even into subalpine areas growing mostly in deciduous woods. Although the taste is slightly bitter when raw, the flesh is firm and cooks well, and this is regarded as a good edible fungus. Somewhat variable in colour, and it may be that the smaller and more orange-coloured *H. rufescens* is best considered as only a form of this species.

AURISCALPIACEAE

Ear Pick-fungus
Auriscalpium vulgare

ID FACT FILE

Fruitbody: With lateral cap and stem. Cap 1–2 cm, kidney-shaped, dark brown, velvety, bearing teeth on underside

Teeth: 1–3 mm long, pinkish-brown. Spores white

Stem: 2–4 cm high, slender, dark brown, bristly

Habitat: On fallen, rotting, often buried pine cones

Season: All year but mainly autumn

Lookalikes: None; habitat, shape and colour are characteristic

An unusual and distinctive species, but rather inconspicuous in the woodland litter and easy to overlook. The lateral, semicircular cap with spines on the underside is unlike that of any other fungus, and the species can hardly be mistaken even when springing from cones which are buried. It usually grows singly, rarely in small groups, from the cones, and is common in suitable habitats in Europe.

POLYPORACEAE

Winter Polypore
Polyporus brumalis

ID FACT FILE

Cap: 2–7 cm across, convex to flat with central depression, deep brown, margin often with fringe of hairs. Flesh tough

Stem: 2–5 cm long, velvety, brown below, paler above

Tubes: Short, slightly decurrent

Pores: 3–4 per mm, angular to elongated, edges often torn, whitish. Spores white

Habitat: On dead branches and twigs, mostly of deciduous trees

Season: Late autumn–spring

Lookalikes: *P. ciliatus*, in summer, is paler brown and with small pores

The small species of *Polyporus* which have a central stem and circular cap have proved to be an area of considerable confusion. Winter Polypore can be distinguished by its dark brown cap and relatively large pores, and occurs in spring and late autumn. It is common throughout Europe except for more northern parts. It is found on dead branches and twigs, mostly of deciduous trees, causing a white rot of the substrate.

POLYPORACEAE

| J | F | M | A | M | J |
| J | A | S | O | N | D |

Dryad's Saddle
Polyporus squamosus

ID FACT FILE

Cap: 12–30 cm across, semi-circular, yellow-brown with dark brown, flat, concentric scales

Stem: Eccentric or lateral, short, blackish at base, apex with a network formed by decurrent pores

Tubes: Whitish, decurrent. Pores large, angular, edges often torn. Spores white

Habitat: On stumps and trunks of dead or dying deciduous trees

Season: Early summer–autumn

Lookalikes: *P. tuberaster* has rougher scales and grows from a large underground sclerotium. *P. mori* is much smaller and grows on gorse stems

A common and highly distinctive species, with a scaly, yellow-ochre cap – hence the other common name 'Scaly Polypore'. This species occurs especially on ash, elm and sycamore, on logs, stumps and even living trunks. It sometimes forms strange, stag-horn like structures if developed in the dark. It may also develop as a parasite, often entering the host where branches have been broken off, and causes a heart rot which can result in the trunk of the tree becoming hollowed out.

POLYPORACEAE

Varied Polypore
Polyporus varius

ID FACT FILE

CAP: 5–10 cm across, flattened, smooth, yellow-brown, finely streaky. Flesh tough

STEM: Short, eccentric or lateral, pale yellowish with blackish base

TUBES: Short, decurrent. Pores cream to pale grey-brown, small. Spores white

HABITAT: On dead stumps and branches of deciduous trees

SEASON: All year, especially late summer–autumn

LOOKALIKES: *P. badius* is much darker brown and has smaller pores. *P. melanopus* is more robust and has stem black throughout

A fairly common species, especially on willow and beech, occurring as a saprophyte on the dead wood and causing a white soft-rot. The stem is black only towards the base, a character which helps to distinguish this species from the related *P. badius* that has a shiny red-brown to purple-black cap, and *P. melanopus* that is dark brown and velvety.

CORIOLACEAE

Many-zoned Polypore
Trametes versicolor

ID FACT FILE

FRUITBODY:
Bracket-like, often in tiers, 3–8 cm across, 1–4 cm wide. Upper surface zoned in various colours, velvety at first, smooth with age. Flesh tough, thin, flexible, whitish. Tubes short, pores small, whitish. Spores white

HABITAT: On dead stumps and logs of various trees

SEASON: All year

LOOKALIKES:
T. pubescens is whitish and lacks coloured zones. *T. hirsutus* is more hairy, less zoned and paler. *T. multicolor* has thicker flesh

One of the commonest of the bracket fungi, often forming large groups. It occurs on a range of hardwoods, including structural timber, and is occasionally found on conifers. The cap is always distinctly zoned, but very variable in colour. It does not change much in appearance on drying, and was once used as jewellery.

CORIOLACEAE

Smoky Polypore
Bjerkandera adusta

ID FACT FILE

FRUITBODY: Partly resupinate, leathery, forming irregularly tiered brackets 3–7 cm across and 1–2 cm wide. Upper surface grey-brown, velvety, margin paler. Lower surface poroid, pores small, smoky-grey, whitish at margin. Flesh whitish to grey. Spores yellowish

HABITAT: On decaying stumps of deciduous trees

SEASON: All year

LOOKALIKES: *B. fumosa* is thicker, with pale brown pores and sweetish smell

A common species, one of the very few polypores which have grey pores and are usually quite easy to recognise. The upper surface is slightly zoned, but much less so than in *Trametes versicolor* (p.171) which also differs in its white pores. It occurs on various deciduous trees, especially beech, either as a saprophyte on dead stumps causing a white soft-rot, or occasionally as a wound parasite on living trees.

CORIOLACEAE

Beech Bracket
Pseudotrametes gibbosa

ID FACT FILE

FRUITBODY:
Bracket-like,
10–20 cm
across, upper
surface whitish,
with concentric
zones, base
often green due
to algal growth.
Flesh tough,
corky, up to 8 cm
thick at base,
whitish. Tubes to
1.5 cm long,
walls thick.
Pores commonly
elongated.
Spores white

HABITAT: On rot-
ten stumps and
logs, especially
of beech

SEASON: All year,
especially
autumn

LOOKALIKES:
Unlikely to be
confused with
other species

This species is widespread and generally
common in Europe. The growth of algae on
the upper surface, especially near the base of
the brackets, is a distinctive feature of it. However, the brackets vary somewhat in form and
thickness, and especially in the form of the
pores which may or may not be markedly elongated. The brackets are tough but annual and
are readily attacked by midge larvae.

CORIOLACEAE

Violet conifer-bracket
Trichaptum abietinum

ID FACT FILE

FRUITBODY: Partly resupinate, usually with well-developed brackets; cap small, 2–3 cm wide, united in rows and tiers. Upper surface hairy, whitish to greyish, zoned. Flesh thin, tough, flexible. Tubes very short, pore surface violet or purple, pores irregular, often torn. Spores white

HABITAT: On stumps, logs and fallen branches of conifers

SEASON: All year

LOOKALIKES: *T. fuscoviolaceum* has underside with irregular teeth

Common on various species of conifer, especially pine, often growing in extensive rows on fallen logs, and easily distinguished by the purple or violet pore layer. It is never parasitic, but occurs on fallen trunks and branches, or on trees damaged by fire, causing a rapid decay of the sapwood. It may also occur on worked timber.

CORIOLACEAE

J	F	M	A	M	J
J	A	S	O	N	D

Blueing Bracket
Postia caesia

ID FACT FILE

Fruitbody:
Bracket-like,
2–7 cm across,
0.5–1 cm thick.
Upper surface
white to greyish,
woolly. Flesh
soft, watery, with
blue-grey tinge.
Tubes white, to
6 mm long;
pores small,
becoming blue-
grey with age or
when bruised.
Spores white

Habitat: On
stumps and logs,
mostly of
conifers

Season: Autumn

Lookalikes:
P. subcaesia, on
deciduous trees

Widely distributed and fairly common,
occurring as a saprophyte on dead coniferous
wood. Easily recognised by the substrate and
the soft, whitish brackets which soon become
distinctly blue or blue-grey. A related species,
P. subcaesia, is similar but has fruitbodies
which are much less distinctly blue and occur
on deciduous trees.

CORIOLACEAE

Bitter Bracket
Postia stiptica

ID FACT FILE

FRUITBODY:
2–8 cm across,
1–3 cm thick at
the base, brac-
ket-like. Upper
surface whitish,
rough and
uneven. Flesh
white, taste
bitter. Tubes to
7 mm long;
pores whitish,
exuding droplets
when fresh.
Spores white

HABITAT: On dead
stumps and logs,
usually of
conifers

SEASON:
Summer–autumn

LOOKALIKES:
P. lactea has
mild taste

Widespread in Europe and generally common, growing singly or in fused tiers. The bitter-tasting flesh is characteristic of the species, and readily separates it from others which are similar in appearance. It is a saprophyte (feeds on dead or decaying organic matter) or rarely a weak parasite. It is found mostly on conifers but occasionally on deciduous trees.

CORIOLACEAE

| J | F | M | A | M | J |
| J | A | S | O | N | D |

Chicken-of-the-Woods
Laetiporus sulphureus

ID FACT FILE

FRUITBODY: Thick, irregular, with separate brackets arising from common base, 15–40 cm across. Upper surface yellow or orange at first with sulphur-yellow margin, fading to whitish with age. Flesh thick, whitish. Pores small, sulphur-yellow when young. Spores white

HABITAT: On stumps and logs of various trees

SEASON: Early summer–autumn

LOOKALIKES: None

One of the most distinctive of the bracket fungi due to its bright yellow and orange colours. With age the colours fade to whitish, and the flesh becomes cheese-like and crumbly. It is parasitic, entering through wounds and causing a brown, cuboidal rot of the heart wood. However, infected trees may live for many years. Often eaten when young and fresh, but can cause allergic reactions.

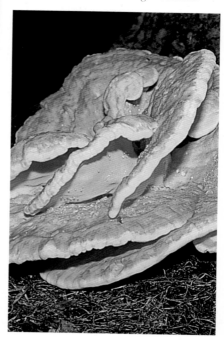

CORIOLACEAE

Giant Polypore
Meripilus giganteus

ID FACT FILE

FRUITBODY: Very large, 50–150 cm across, comprising numerous brackets fused at the base. Brackets 10–25 cm across, fan-shaped, narrowed below, yellow-brown, upper surface with darker zones. Flesh whitish, bruising black when damaged. Pores very small, whitish. Spores white

HABITAT: At base of trunks and on roots of various deciduous trees

SEASON: Summer–autumn

LOOKALIKES: *Grifola frondosa* may resemble small fruitbodies of *M. gigantea* but does not bruise black

A common and widely distributed species in Europe, readily recognised on account of its habit and very large size. Developed mostly on the roots of trees, it causes an active white rot which is confined to the base of the trunk and may lead to the fall of the tree. Not poisonous, but inedible on account of the tough flesh and unpleasant taste.

CORIOLACEAE

Birch Polypore
Piptoporus betulinus

ID FACT FILE

FRUITBODY:
Bracket-like with narrowed attachment, 10–20 cm across, 3–8 cm thick, at first rounded, soon hoof-shaped, upper surface convex, pale brown, smooth, skin separable. Flesh firm, white. Pores small, whitish. Spores white

HABITAT: On trunks of birch

SEASON: All year

LOOKALIKES: None

A very common polypore, found on most dead and dying trunks of birch, sometimes many on a tree. It attacks both the heartwood and the sapwood, and eventually causes the top of the tree to fall out. The firm flesh of this species is ideal for stropping razors and was once used for this purpose; indeed, it has the alternative common name of Razor-strop Fungus.

CORIOLACEAE

J F M A M J
J A S O N D

Maze-gill
Daedalea quercina

ID FACT FILE

FRUITBODY: Tough, corky, forming semicircular to hoof-shaped brackets 5–15 cm across. Upper surface pale brownish, with concentric ridges, smooth. Flesh 3–6 cm thick, wood-coloured, firm. Tubes 1.5–2.5 cm long. Pores elongated, maze-like

HABITAT: On stumps of oak and sweet chestnut

SEASON: All year

LOOKALIKES: Blushing Bracket (p.181) may have maze-like pores, but is thinner fleshed and pores redden when bruised

The tough, thick-fleshed brackets have gill-like pores and should be easy to recognise. They may be perennial, and can be found at any time of the year. Though most frequent on oak, like many oak fungi they also occur on sweet chestnut, causing a red-brown cubical rot. This species was once known as the Curry-comb Fungus, the fruitbodies being used for cleaning down horses with skin too tender for an ordinary curry-comb. It was once common, but is now apparently much less frequent in many areas.

CORIOLACEAE

Blushing Bracket

Daedaleopsis confragosa

Once known as *Trames rubescens*, the epithet and the common name referring to the distinct reddish colour which rapidly develops when the pores are bruised. This is a common species, usually very regular in shape when fully developed, but very variable with regard to the form of the pores which may be gill-like in some forms. It causes a white soft-rot of the substrate. Inedible on account of the tough, unpleasant flesh.

ID FACT FILE

FRUITBODY: Forming semicirclar brackets 4–9 cm across. Upper surface zoned and with fine, irregular radial ridges. Flesh whitish, 1.5–3.5 cm thick at base. Pores variable in form, usually somewhat radially elongated, whitish, bruising red. Spores white

HABITAT: On dead logs and branches, especially of willow and birch

SEASON: Autumn

LOOKALIKES: Mazegill (p.180) has thicker fruitbodies, on oak

CORIOLACEAE

Root Fomes
Heterobasidion annosum

ID FACT FILE

FRUITBODY:
Resupinate or
forming a brac-
ket, up to 15 cm
across, 2–3 cm
thick, surface
uneven, brown to
orange-brown,
margin white.
Flesh firm, tough,
whitish to cream.
Pores small,
white. Spores
white

HABITAT: Base of
living trunks of
conifers, some-
times other trees

SEASON: All year

LOOKALIKES: None;
the hard flesh
and white margin
are distinctive

A serious parasite of conifers, forming brackets at the trunk base and on the roots. This species is especially damaging to plantation conifers but also occurs in native forests, causing a serious white heart rot of the host trunk. Brackets are perennial and may be found throughout the year. The firm, hard flesh and white margin make the species distinctive.

CORIOLACEAE

Tinder Fungus
Fomes fomentarius

Common in Europe, especially on beech, forming hard, hoof-shaped perennial fruitbodies growing solitary or in tiers on living and dead trees, and causing a white soft-rot of the heartwood. In Britain it is most frequent in Scotland where it occurs on birch; it is rarer but apparently spreading in S England, where it occurs on birch, beech and sycamore.

ID FACT FILE

| J | F | M | A | M | J |
| J | A | S | O | N | D |

FRUITBODY: A solid, hoof-like bracket 10–30 cm across, 5–20 cm thick. Upper surface with a hard crust, greyish, with concentric grooves. Flesh tough, pale brown. Tubes brown, in annual layers. Pores small, greybrown. Spores yellowish

HABITAT: Mostly on beech and birch

SEASON: Perennial

LOOKALIKES: *Ganoderma adspersum* (p.186) has brown crust, and whitish pore layer which bruises brown. *Phellinus igniarius* has dark brown flesh

HYMENOCHAETACEAE

| J | F | M | A | M | J |
| J | A | S | O | N | D |

Large Pine Polypore
Phaeolus schweinitzii

ID FACT FILE

FRUITBODY: Irregular in shape, bracket-like or circular, usually stalked, 10–30 cm across, soft and spongy when fresh. Upper surface roughly hairy, yellow-brown to dark brown, with yellow margin. Flesh rusty-brown, fibrous. Pore surface olive-yellow then rusty. Spores pale yellowish

HABITAT: On roots and trunks of conifers

SEASON: Autumn

LOOKALIKES: Some *Inonotus* species

Fairly common, usually on pine. This species is parasitic, usually on the roots, penetrating the heartwood and causing a brown, cuboidal rot. It can occur on many conifers, but is most common on pines and spruces. Fruitbodies are annual, and continue to fruit on the dead tree. The soft, spongy flesh becomes light and brittle when dry.

CORIOLACEAE

Elm Bracket
Rigidoporus ulmarius

ID FACT FILE

FRUITBODY: Perennial, bracket-like, often very large, to 1 m or more across, upper surface whitish to yellowish, often lumpy and irregular. Margin blunt. Flesh whitish, tough, woody. Tubes to 6 mm long, in annual layers, orange-brown; pores very small, pale orange-brown. Spores white

HABITAT: On trunks, stumps and roots of elm

SEASON: All year

LOOKALIKES: The large size and orange-brown pores are distinctive

Common in parts of southern Britain, but less so elsewhere in Europe. It causes a serious butt rot of elm, and brackets often develop inside old hollow stumps. Perennial, sometimes growing for 10 or 15 years while the food supply continues, and reaching a very large size. Indeed, the largest known specimen of a bracket-fungus belongs to this species.

GANODERMATACEAE

Artist's Fungus
Ganoderma adspersum

ID FACT FILE

FRUITBODY: A large, solid bracket, up to 60 cm across. Upper surface a dull grey-brown crust with concentric grooves. Flesh tough, rust-brown, to 10 cm thick. Tubes in annual layers; pores whitish, readily bruising brown. Spores brown

HABITAT: Common on beech, sometimes other trees, causing rot

SEASON: Perennial

LOOKALIKES: *G. applanatum* has thinner bracket with narrow margin, and white flecks in flesh

Very common, growing on various deciduous trees and causing a serious heart rot which is slow to develop but will eventually kill the tree. The pore surface is whitish but immediately bruises brown so that it is possible to draw or write on it, hence the common name. However, other species, notably *G. applanatum*, show a similar bruising.

GANODERMATACEAE

Shiny Bracket
Ganoderma lucidum

ID FACT FILE

FRUITBODY:
Stalked, with shiny red-brown or purple-brown crust. Cap semi-circular or kidney-shaped, 6–20 cm across, with lateral stalk, surface concentrically zoned and grooved, margin paler when young. Stalk variable, up to 20 cm long, 1–3 cm thick. Pores small, whitish at first then brown. Spores rusty

HABITAT: On trunks and roots of deciduous trees

SEASON: All year

LOOKALIKES:
G. carnosum, on conifers. *G. resinaceum* usually lacks stalk

A well-known and distinctive but uncommon species easily recognised by the stalk and shiny reddish-brown surface. Widely distributed, occurring most often on oak and causing a white rot. In China, a closely related species, *G. sinensis*, is much used in medicine, as a supposed cure for some cancers and as a general tonic.

FISTULINACEAE

Beefsteak Fungus
Fistulina hepatica

ID FACT FILE

FRUITBODY:
10–30 cm
across, fleshy,
soft, tongue-like,
narrowed behind,
often with a
short stalk,
blood-red to red-
brown. Upper
surface rough-
ened. Flesh
exuding reddish
juice when cut.
Tubes separate,
reddish; pores
round, reddish-
cream or yellow-
ish. Spores
pinkish

HABITAT: On
trunks, usually of
oak or sweet
chestnut

SEASON:
Summer–autumn

LOOKALIKES: None

A distinctive fungus, the flesh having a strong
resemblance to beefsteak, even exuding a
reddish fluid, hence the common name. It is
not uncommon, occurring on living oaks,
sometimes other trees, causing a brown rot. It
is an edible species, but usually has a rather
unpleasant, acidulous taste from tannins in the
tree, and is not recommended.

HYMENOCHAETACEAE

J	F	M	A	M	J
J	A	S	O	N	D

Brown Funnel Polypore
Coltricia perennis

ID FACT FILE

Cap: 2–6 cm across, shallow funnel-shaped, finely velvety, with tawny and rusty-brown concentric zones

Stem: 1–3 cm high, cylindric, rust-brown. Flesh tough, thin, tawny-brown

Tubes: Short, slightly decurrent, pores small. Spores yellow-brown

Habitat: Usually on old burnt sites on heaths

Season: Late summer–winter

Lookalikes: *C. cinnamomea* has larger spores. *Onnia tomentosa*, rare, in coniferous woods, has unzoned cap

Widespread in Europe, but not common, occuring in various habitats, frequently on old burnt sites but also on sandy soil in woods. The velvety, zoned cap, tough flesh and central stem should make it easy to distinguish except from *C. cinnamomea*, although the latter, differing only in larger spores, is not considered a distinct species by all authors.

HYMENOCHAETACEAE

J	F	M	A	M	J
J	A	S	O	N	D

Weeping Oak Bracket

Inonotus dryadeus

ID FACT FILE

FRUITBODY:
Bracket-like,
15–40 cm
across, up to
12 cm thick,
corky; upper sur-
face pale greyish-
brown becoming
darker, margin
broad, rounded,
weeping reddish-
yellow droplets.
Pores small,
becoming rust-
brown. Flesh
rusty-brown,
fibrous, soft but
tough. Spores
whitish

HABITAT: At base
of oak trunks

SEASON: All year

LOOKALIKES: None

An uncommon but rather distinctive species almost always found at the base of oak trunks, though also reported from sweet chestnut. The weeping margin, leaving spots on the upper surface, is also characteristic. The species is parasitic, causing a white butt rot confined to the heartwood but not causing serious harm to the tree for many years.

HYMENOCHAETACEAE

J	F	M	A	M	J
J	A	S	O	N	D

Hairy Bracket
Inonotus hispidus

ID FACT FILE

FRUITBODY: Forming brackets 10–25 cm across, 3–8 cm thick, upper surface distinctly bristly-hairy, brown to dark brown. Flesh soft, rusty-brown. Pores small, at first ochraceous becoming rust-brown. Spores yellow-brown

HABITAT: Parasitic on various trees such as ash, elm and especially apple

SEASON: Summer–autumn

LOOKALIKES: *Phaeolus schweinitzii* (p.184) may look similar when old, but occurs on conifers

This fungus is a parasite, infecting the host tree through wounds and causing a spongy white rot of the heartwood. Brackets develop on the trunk and branches. It is an uncommon but distinctive species, recognised by the soft flesh, bright rusty brown colour and shaggy surface. It forms annual fruitbodies. Old brackets become dry, hard and blackish.

HYMENOCHAETACEAE

Alder Bracket
Inonotus radiatus

J	F	M	A	M	J
J	A	S	O	N	D

ID FACT FILE

FRUITBODY: Bracket-like, growing in tiers, 4–7 cm across, 2–4 cm thick at the base. Upper surface tawny-brown, with bright yellowish margin, finely velvety at first. Flesh yellow-brown, fibrous, firm, hard when dry. Pores small, yellow-brown to rusty, surface glancing when viewed at an angle. Spores pale yellow

HABITAT: On trunks of deciduous trees, usually alder and birch

SEASON: Summer–autumn

LOOKALIKES: *I. nodulosus*, common in parts of Europe on beech

An uncommon species, mostly found on dead or weakened trunks of alder, more rarely on birch or other trees. It forms distinct brackets which are often developed in dense tiers on standing trunks, and is an important cause of heart rot of alder. As with other species of this and related genera, the brown flesh turns dark with alkali solution.

HYMENOCHAETACEAE

Grey Fire-bracket

Phellinus igniarius

ID FACT FILE

FRUITBODY:
Bracket-like,
10–30 cm
across, 5–15 cm
thick, hoof-
shaped, hard,
woody. Upper
surface with con-
centric grooves,
dark brown to
grey-brown, later
blackish; margin
rounded, pale
brown, velvety.
Flesh rusty-
brown. Pores
small, rusty-
brown

HABITAT: Parasitic
on willows,
sometimes other
deciduous trees

SEASON: Mostly
spring–autumn

LOOKALIKES:
P. nigricans, on
birch

Widely distributed and generally frequent in
Europe and also in America. It is a parasite,
causing a white heart rot, and forming perennial brackets which can be found at any time of
the year but are most actively growing from
spring to autumn. It is most common on
willows, but also occurs on alder and apple,
and occasionally on other deciduous trees.

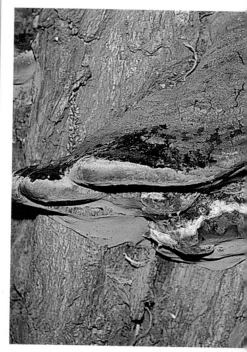

HYMENOCHAETACEAE

Rigid Leather-bracket
Hymenochaete rubiginosa

| J | F | M | A | M | J |
| J | A | S | O | N | D |

ID FACT FILE

FRUITBODY: Partly resupinate, with brackets forming long rows and often dense tiers. Bracket 1–2 cm wide, up to 7 cm across, margin wavy, rather rigid, upper surface red-brown to date, with concentric zones, soon smooth. Fertile surface rust-brown. Flesh thin, rust-brown. Spores pale yellowish

HABITAT: On rotten stumps of oak and sweet chestnut

SEASON: All year

LOOKALIKES: *H. tabacina*, tobacco-brown, on willow and hazel

The species occurs on barkless stumps and trunks and is confined to oak and sweet chestnut. It can often be found in the same place for many years, causing a white pocket-rot. The rather rigid, red-brown brackets make this a distinctive species similar only to *H. tabacina* which differs in colour and substrate.

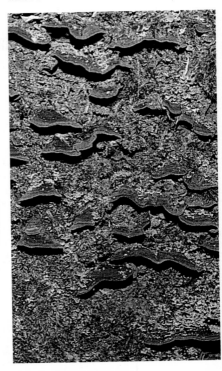

STEREACEAE

| J | F | M | A | M | J |
| J | A | S | O | N | D |

Wrinkled Leather-bracket
Stereum rugosum

ID FACT FILE

FRUITBODY: Tough, leathery, mostly resupinate and with at most only narrow brackets; upper surface of bracket hairy, ochre-brown to greyish-brown, irregular in form. Fertile surface often stratified, buff or pinkish-buff, bleeding a red juice when scratched. Flesh rather thick. Spores white

HABITAT: On branches and logs of deciduous trees

SEASON: Throughout the year

LOOKALIKES: *S. gausapatum*, on oak, is thinner, forms distinct white-margined brackets and has copious red juice; *S. sanguineum* is on conifers

One of several bleeding *Stereum* species, recognised by the lack of well-developed brackets and the fairly thick, often stratified flesh. It is a common species, occurring on various deciduous trees, especially beech and oak. It grows as a saprophyte but may also be parasitic. It develops a white 'pipe rot', and is the cause of a serious decay of timber.

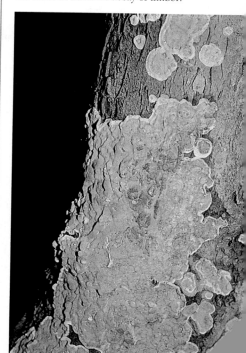

STEREACEAE

Hairy Leather-bracket
Stereum hirsutum

J	F	M	A	M	J
J	A	S	O	N	D

ID FACT FILE

FRUITBODY: Bracket-like, 3–7 cm across, upper surface hairy, pale yellowish-grey, faintly zoned, margin wavy. Flesh thin, tough, leathery. Fertile surface smooth, bright yellow-orange, fading with age, not bleeding when cut. Spores white

HABITAT: Mostly on dead stumps and logs of deciduous trees

SEASON: All year

LOOKALIKES: Distinct, when fresh, in bright yellow-orange colours

A very common species, the commonest member of the genus throughout Europe. It occurs usually on fallen trunks and branches, rotting the sapwood, but is occasionally parasitic. It is variable in form, usually with well-developed brackets, but can sometimes be mostly resupinate, especially if growing on the underside of logs. The uncommon *Trenella aurantia* is parasitic on this species.

STEREACEAE

Silver-leaf Bracket
Chondrostereum purpureum

ID FACT FILE

FRUITBODY:
Resupinate, sometimes in extensive patches, with upturned, bracket-like margin, 2–4 cm across, often developed in tiers. Upper side whitish or greyish, hairy. Lower surface purplish, smooth. Spores white

HABITAT: On logs and stumps of deciduous trees, also parasitic, especially on rosaceous trees, causing silver-leaf disease

SEASON: Summer–autumn

LOOKALIKES: Some species of *Amylostereum*, which are on conifers

Occurs on a range of hardwood substrates, though frequently on birch. It is easy to recognise, at least in fresh condition, by the purple to violet-brown fertile surface. Though frequently a saprophyte, this species causes the important silver-leaf disease of plum trees and other rosaceous species. This affects the foliage, causing the leaf surface to develop a silvery sheen and trees may die in 2–3 years.

MERULIACEAE

Jelly Rot
Merulius tremellosus

ID FACT FILE

FRUITBODY: Wide-spreading, resupinate with bracket-like margin, in tiers. Bracket 2–7 cm across, gelatinous, upper surface woolly, whitish, often with pinkish margin. Pore surface orange-yellow to pinkish, with a network of veins forming shallow, irregular pores. Flesh thin, pale yellowish to whitish. Spores white

HABITAT: On stumps and logs of various trees, especially beech

SEASON: All year

LOOKALIKES: Some *Serpula* species, but these are less bracket-like and have yellow spores

Widely distributed in Europe, occurring as a saprophyte on rotten wood of both broadleaved trees and conifers. A distinctive fungus with well-developed, soft, flexible brackets having small, shallow, irregular pores and unlikely to be confused with other species. Fruitbodies may be found in most seasons, but are most frequent in autumn and early winter.

MERULIACEAE

Vein Crust
Phlebia radiata

ID FACT FILE

FRUITBODY:
Effused, forming irregular, encrusting patches 2–10 cm across, surface strongly radially wrinkled, with irregular, lumpy centre, greyish-orange with bright orange margin. Margin fimbriate, free. Spores white

HABITAT: On stumps and trunks, mostly of deciduous trees

SEASON: All year

LOOKALIKES:
P. rufa may be similar in colour but has almost poroid fertile surface

A common species, usually easy to recognise by the bright orange colours. However, it is somewhat variable in form and colour; the orange may fade with age and a white form is also known. For this reason, *P. radiata* has received several names. The commonly seen name, *Phlebia merismoides,* is one of its synonyms.

THELEPHORACEAE

Earth-fan
Thelephora terrestris

ID FACT FILE

FRUITBODY: Variable in form, commonly fan-like, 2–6 cm across, with irregular, torn margin. Fertile surface chocolate-brown. Upper surface felty

HABITAT: On the ground, roots and debris in woods, on sandy soil

SEASON: Late summer–autumn

LOOKALIKES: *T. penicillata*, more cushion-like with fine, short branches

Widespread and fairly common, especially in coniferous woods, occurring on the soil or frequently creeping over roots, branches and plant stems, sometimes covering extensive areas. The fan-shaped or rosette-like fruit-bodies are distinctive, unlike those of other *Thelephora* species which are usually much more branched or coral-like.

AURICULARIACEAE

J	F	M	A	M	J
J	A	S	O	N	D

Jew's Ear
Auricularia auricula-judae

ID FACT FILE

FRUITBODY: Ear-shaped or irregular, 3–8 cm across, gelatinous, drying hard. Outer surface reddish-brown, finely hairy. Inner surface grey-brown, somewhat wrinkled. Spores white

HABITAT: On dead branches of deciduous trees, especially elder

SEASON: All year

LOOKALIKES: Some *Peziza* species, but these have brittle, non-gelatinous flesh

The ear-like, gelatinous fruitbodies are edible and treated as a delicacy in some parts of the world. The species occurs on a range of trees but is most common on elder. The common name is a corruption of 'Judas's ear', referring to Judas Iscariot who supposedly hanged himself upon an elder tree after his betrayal of Christ to the Pharisees.

AURICULARIACEAE

Tripe Fungus
Auricularia mesenterica

ID FACT FILE

FRUITBODY: Irregular, gelatinous, spreading and often bracket-like. Upper surface hairy, zoned, grey-brown, margin whitish, lobed. Lower surface purple-red, with whitish bloom, irregularly lobed and wrinkled

HABITAT: On rotten logs and stumps of deciduous trees, especially elm and beech

SEASON: All year

LOOKALIKES: Silver-leaf Bracket (p.197) may appear similar but is less lobed and wrinkled and not gelatinous

Common in most areas and usually easy to recognise by its hairy brackets and the lobed underside which may be rather gut-like in appearance, hence the specific name. It has a rather soft, gelatinous flesh which, as in most jelly fungi, becomes hard and rigid when dry. Not poisonous, but unpleasant in taste and texture and not recommended for eating.

DACRYMYCETACEAE

Pale Antler-fungus
Calocera pallidospathulata

ID FACT FILE

FRUITBODY: Gelatinous, variable in colour, pale to dark orange, 4–12 mm high, stalked. Fertile head irregular in shape

HABITAT: In swarms on rotten branches of both deciduous and coniferous trees

SEASON: Autumn

LOOKALIKES: *C. glossoides* is more flame-shaped, with vertical grooves and never occurs in swarms

The species has a unique and interesting history. It was unknown to science before 1976 when it was described from England. Since then it has spread rapidly and is now common in parts of S England, where it occurs on all kinds of branches; it has also recently been recorded on the Continent. Its origins remain uncertain.

DACRYMYCETACEAE

Jelly Antler-fungus
Calocera viscosa

J	F	M	A	M	J
J	A	S	O	N	D

ID FACT FILE

FRUITBODY:
Orange-yellow,
2–8 cm high,
branched, antler-
like, rubbery,
rather slimy,
base-rooting.
Spores yellowish

HABITAT: On
rotting stumps of
conifers

SEASON: Late
summer–early
winter

LOOKALIKES: Some
Clavaria species,
which are fragile
and not on
stumps. Other
Calocera species
are rarely
branched

Very common, but somewhat variable in form.
The fruitbody is usually branched, with the
branches also forked, and may grow singly or
in clusters. The texture of the flesh, sticky, firm
and pliable, distinguishes it from superficially
similar species of Fairy-club fungi. A rare
white form has been called var. *cavarae*.

DACRYMYCETACEAE

J	F	M	A	M	J
J	A	S	O	N	D

ID FACT FILE

FRUITBODY: Gelatinous, rather soft when fresh, yellow to orange, irregular in size and form, mostly cushion-like, 3–8 mm across

HABITAT: On dead wood of all kinds

SEASON: All year

LOOKALIKES: Some other *Dacrymyces* species, differentiated only on microscopic characters. Young *Tremella mesenterica* (p.207) may also be similar

Common Jelly Spot
Dacrymyces stillatus

Very common, to be found on all kinds of rotting wood in damp places, including worked timber such as posts, rails and boards. The soft, gelatinous, orange-yellow cushion-like fruitbodies are characteristic, although there are several other less common species of *Dacrymyces* which may be confused with it.

TREMELLACEAE

Black Brain Fungus

Exidia glandulosa

ID FACT FILE

FRUITBODY:
2–6 cm across, gelatinous, blackish, translucent, fertile surface and underside both with small warts, under surface velvety. Spores white

HABITAT: Dead logs and branches of deciduous trees, especially of oak

SEASON: All year, mostly summer–late autumn

LOOKALIKES:
E. recisa, on willows, is more orange-brown, and smooth. *E. saccharina* is also brown but occurs on pine

In some areas, this fungus is also known as Black Witches' Butter, on account of the soft, gelatinous flesh. It is common, occurring on various broadleaved trees but especially on oak. The rather top-shaped fruitbodies have both the fertile surface and the underside bearing small warts. The individual fruitbodies often amalgamate to form large, irregular masses.

TREMELLACEAE

Yellow Brain Fungus
Tremella mesenterica

ID FACT FILE

FRUITBODY:
2–9 cm across, gelatinous, soft, bright orange-yellow, much convoluted and irregular in form. Hard when dry. Spores white

HABITAT: On *Peniophora* species on dead branches of deciduous wood

SEASON: All year, especially autumn–spring

LOOKALIKES: The similar but much less common *T. aurantia* occurs on Hairy Leather-bracket (p.196)

A very common and distinctive species, found on various branches but especially on gorse. It is brain-like with shapeless lobes, and is bright orange-yellow in colour. Like all *Tremella* species, it occurs as a parasite on another fungus, in this case on various species of *Peniophora*. On gorse, it occurs on *P. incarnata*, although the fruitbody of the *Peniophora* is not always evident.

LYCOPERDACEAE

Common Puffball
Lycoperdon perlatum

ID FACT FILE

FRUITBODY:
4–9 cm high,
2.5–5 cm
across, rounded
above, with
stem-like base,
at first whitish,
soon yellowish-
brown; surface of
upper part
densely covered
with fragile, coni-
cal warts which
soon become
rubbed away to
leave a distinct
net-like pattern.
Opening by a
small pore.
Spore mass
olive-brown.
Sterile base
spongy

HABITAT: Woods

SEASON:
Summer–autumn

LOOKALIKES:
L. foetidum is
darker and has
spines in small
groups, and
united at their
tips

The commonest of the puffballs, usually growing in groups and found in various kinds of woodland. It is most easily recognised by the conical spines which leave a net-like pattern when rubbed away. The fruitbodies are edible when young, whilst still white inside, but are not recommended. In common with various species of puffball, the spore mass of this fungus was once used as a styptic.

LYCOPERDACEAE

Stump Puffball
Lycoperdon pyriforme

ID FACT FILE

FRUITBODY:
2–5 cm high,
1.5–4 cm
across, rounded
above, often with
central boss, and
with a distinct
stem-like base.
Surface scurfy
with fine spines
which are soon
lost leaving an
almost smooth
wall, opening by
a small apical
pore. Spore
mass olive-brown
at maturity. Base
with branching,
white mycelial
cords

HABITAT: In clus-
ters on rotten
logs, stumps and
roots

SEASON:
Summer–autumn

LOOKALIKES: Other
puffballs are
mostly less
smooth, not on
wood and lack
white cords at
base

Common, the only European species of puffball which grows on wood. The white strands
of mycelium at the base are also characteristic,
and a useful aid to identification if the fruitbodies are growing from buried wood thus
appearing to be on the soil. The fruitbodies are
reported to contain a substance which is effective against some forms of cancer. Edible when
young and still white inside.

LYCOPERDACEAE

Meadow Puffball
Vascellum pratense

ID FACT FILE

FRUITBODY:
1.5–4 cm high,
2–4 cm across,
flat-topped at
maturity, surface
scurfy, at first
with small spines
which are soon
lost, whitish at
first later grey-
brown. Opening
irregular. Sterile
base present,
separated from
the fertile part by
a distinct skin-
like diaphragm.
Spores olive-
brown

HABITAT: In
various kinds of
grassland

SEASON: Early
summer–late
autumn

LOOKALIKES: *Hand-
kea utriformis*
(p.213), in simi-
lar habitats, is
much larger

Very common throughout Europe. It occurs in
most types of grassland, though preferring
drier habitats, and can tolerate the addition of
artificial fertilisers to the soil. Old fruitbodies,
with spores lost, look somewhat like a cigar
butt, the diaphragm (a wall which separates
the spore mass from the sterile base and is a
feature of the genus) being clearly evident at
that stage.

LYCOPERDACEAE

Black Bovist
Bovista nigrescens

ID FACT FILE

FRUITBODY: Sub-globose, 4–6 cm across, loosely attached, soon free and rolled by the wind. Outer surface at first white, flaking away to expose dark, purple-brown then blackish-brown and shiny inner wall. Opening by a large, irregular pore. Sterile base lacking. Spore mass dark purple-brown

HABITAT: Grass-land, on moors, in meadows, parks

SEASON: Late summer–autum, old fruitbodies persisting

LOOKALIKES: *B. plumbea* is smaller, lead-grey

Readily distinguished from true puffballs by the lack of a sterile base, and the mode of opening. This species is widespread in Europe, occurring in lowland pastures as well as in alpine regions. Fruitbodies have been discovered in prehistoric dwellings at various sites in England and Scot-land, where they were possibly used as insula-tion against draughts. Other likely uses for this species were as a styptic and as tinder.

LYCOPERDACEAE

Pestle-shaped Puffball
Handkea excipuliformis

ID FACT FILE

FRUITBODY:
9–18 cm high, pestle-shaped, head 5–10 cm across. Surface when young finely spiny and granular, soon becoming smooth, whitish then pale buff to grey-brown; wall papery, splitting irregularly at the apex at maturity and opening widely. Stalk cylindric or broader below, often curved, to 5 cm thick. Spore mass dark olive-brown when mature

HABITAT: Woods, woodland edge

SEASON: Summer–autumn

LOOKALIKES: Large specimens of Common Puffball (p.208) have small, regular pore and surface distinctly spiny, later with network pattern

Widespread and frequent in places, *Handkea excipuliformis* is easily recognised by its distinctive shape and large size. This is typically a woodland species, sometimes occurring in parks, but rarely found in grassland. The sterile stalk may persist for months after the spores have been shed and the head has disintegrated. Like other puffballs, this is a good edible species whilst the flesh remains white.

LYCOPERDACEAE

J	F	M	A	M	J
J	A	S	O	N	D

Scaly Meadow Puffball
Handkea utriformis

ID FACT FILE

FRUITBODY:
5–15 cm across, subglobose with a short, stout stem-like base. Surface at first white, later cream to pale brown, covered when young with coarse pyramidal warts which are lost as the fruit-body matures. Wall finally thin, parchment-like, opening broadly and irregularly above. Spore mass soon yellow-green then dark olive-brown at maturity

HABITAT:
Meadows

SEASON:
Summer–autumn

LOOKALIKES: Small specimens of Giant Puffball (p.214) have smooth surface and lack sterile base

Frequent in meadows and pastures throughout Europe, even occurring into subalpine regions. The species can be readily recognised when young by the pyramidal warts, and later by its size and the presence of a stem-like base. Old fruitbodies may persist through the winter until the following spring. The fruitbodies are edible when young. The dried fruitbodies of this species have been used to produce 'amadou', used as a tinder or in medicine.

LYCOPERDACEAE

Giant Puffball
Calvatia gigantea

ID FACT FILE

FRUITBODY: Very large, commonly 20–50 cm across, rarely to 80 cm, subglobose or rather flattened, surface when young whitish, soft-leathery, sterile base lacking. At first white inside, spore mass at maturity olive-brown to dark-brown

HABITAT: Grass, parks, copses

SEASON: Summer–autumn

LOOKALIKES: Unmistakable when fresh and mature

One of the largest fungi in the world, unmistakable in appearance, well known and sought after as an excellent edible species. It is also probably the world's most prolific fungus, each fruitbody producing over 7,000,000,000,000 spores. Young fruitbodies whilst still white inside are delicious. It has had various other uses, for example as tinder, and in beekeeping, smouldering fruitbodies being placed beneath the hive to calm the bees. It is also a source of the anti-cancer drug calvacin.

GEASTRACEAE

Striated Earth-star
Geastrum striatum

ID FACT FILE

FRUITBODY: At first closed, then splitting into rays, outer surface encrusted with debris. 3.5–6.5 cm across when expanded. Spore sac 1.0–2.5 cm across, grey-brown, stalked and with a distinctive basal collar. Stalk 3–6 mm high, sometimes sheathed at the base by a ring-like zone. Mouth conical, grooved, 2–5 mm high. Spores dark yellow-brown

HABITAT: In woods, parks, gardens, often on chalky soil

SEASON: Late summer–autumn

LOOKALIKES: *G. pectinatum* and the smaller *G. schmidelii* lack basal collar to the spore sac

Widely distributed, and one of the commonest earth-stars in Britain and Europe. It occurs in a range of habitats, including woods, parks and gardens, especially on rich or chalky soil, and is also found growing in groups. It is easy to recognise by the stalked spore sac, best seen in dried fruitbodies, which unlike other earth-stars has a basal collar. The smooth spore sac with grooved, conical mouth and the encrusted outer surface are also characteristic.

GEASTRACEAE

Common Earth-star
Geastrum triplex

J	F	M	A	M	J
J	A	S	O	N	D

ID FACT FILE

FRUITBODY: Onion-shaped at first, soon splitting into 5–7 rays which arch downwards to expose the fawn to pale buff spore sac. Expanded fruitbody 4–12 cm across, outer surface not encrusted. Spore sac unstalked, 2.5–3.5 cm across with single, fringed pore at the top. Inner layer commonly splitting around the spore-sac and turning upwards to form a distinct collar

HABITAT: On well-drained, calcareous soil, in woods or open areas

SEASON: Summer–late autumn

LOOKALIKES: *G. lageniforme* is smaller and rarer and lacks the collar around the spore sac

One of the most common and also one of the largest of the earth-stars, widely distributed in Europe and indeed throughout temperate and subtropical areas. Its large size and the presence of a distinct collar around the spore sac in most collections make it easy to recognise. The onion-shaped unexpanded fruitbodies are also distinctive, similar to but larger than those of the rare *G. lageniforme*.

SCLERODERMATACEAE

J	F	M	A	M	J
J	A	S	O	N	D

Common Earthball
Scleroderma citrinum

ID FACT FILE

FRUITBODY:
5–12 cm across, rounded to rather depressed, lacking a stem-like base. Wall up to 5 mm thick, tough, surface yellowish to yellow-orange, usually with coarse scales. Spore mass greyish, with white veins, later purple-black, odour unpleasant

HABITAT: Woods and heaths, on acid soils

SEASON: Late summer–autumn

LOOKALIKES:
S. verrucosum and *S. areolatum* have smaller scales, and a stem-like base. *S. bovista* has a thin, almost smooth surface

This is the commonest of the earthballs, found throughout Europe and also in N America. Though used at times to adulterate truffles, this is a somewhat poisonous fungus if ingested in large quantities, and should never be eaten at any stage of its development. An uncommon bolete, *Boletus parasiticus*, can sometimes be found growing on the fruitbodies of the Common Earthball.

young fruitbodies (above)
old, dehisced fruitbody (below)

NIDULARIACEAE

Trumpet Bird's-nest
Cyathus olla

ID FACT FILE

FRUITBODY:
Gregarious,
1–1.5 cm high,
bell- or trumpet-
shaped, at first
closed, margin
flared, base
tapered and nar-
row, outer sur-
face felty,
yellow-brown,
inner surface
whitish-grey,
smooth, contain-
ing several egg-
like peridioles
which contain
the spores

HABITAT: On soil
and debris in gar-
dens, allotments

SEASON:
Spring–late
autumn

LOOKALIKES:
Grooved Bird's-
nest (p.219) is
shaggy, striate
on the inner sur-
face and is less
flared

One of the commonest of the bird's-nest fungi,
most often seen in cultivated areas such as gardens and allotments. It is easy to recognise by
the flared margin and smooth inner surface. The
species occurs throughout Europe and is
also present in N America and in southern
temperate regions. The peridioles, usually
8–10 in number, are comparatively large,
2–3 mm across. The rare *C. stercoreus*, on sand
dunes, is also smooth inside but has a shaggy
outer surface and is not flared.

NIDULARIACEAE

Grooved Bird's-nest
Cyathus striatus

ID FACT FILE

FRUITBODY: An
inverted cone,
1–1.5 cm high,
6–10 mm
across, surface
shaggy, dark red-
dish-brown, at
first closed by a
whitish skin
which soon rup-
tures. Inner sur-
face with distinct
vertical furrows,
pale greyish,
shiny, containing
whitish, egg-like
peridioles each
1–2 mm across

HABITAT: On rot-
ten wood, usually
in woodland litter

SEASON:
Spring–autumn

LOOKALIKES: *C.
stercoreus*, on
sand-dunes, has
smooth inner
surface

Common and widespread in Europe and
throughout temperate regions, often growing
in large numbers amongst debris in woodlands.
The shaggy outer surface and grooved inner
surface are distinctive. The peridioles each
have a fine, thread-like attachment by which,
when splashed out, they readily attach to vegetation. This and other bird's-nest fungi have
long been regarded as a curiosity and have
folk-names such as 'fairy goblets', 'corn bells'
and 'siller cups'.

SPHAEROBOLACEAE

Shooting Star
Sphaerobolus stellatus

ID FACT FILE

FRUITBODY: Small, 1.5–2.5 mm across, whitish to yellow, globose, wall 4-layered, splitting at maturity into teeth which tend to give a star-like pattern. Inner wall pale orange, cup-like, containing a single spherical peridiole, suddenly everted to catapult the peridiole into the air. Peridiole reddish-brown, containing spores

HABITAT: Gregarious, on sticks, leaves etc., mostly in woods

SEASON: All year

LOOKALIKES: None

The species is common in places but is inconspicuous and easily overlooked. However, the tiny, densely clustered whitish to orange fruitbodies, star-shaped after dehiscence, are unmistakable. The single spore-bearing peridiole is shot away, using osmotic pressure to rapidly evert the receptacle, to a distance of up to 5 m. It is a unique method of spore dispersal to which the common name, as well as the alternative, Cannonball Fungus, aptly refers.

PHALLACEAE

Dog Stinkhorn
Mutinus caninus

ID FACT FILE

FRUITBODY:
8–12 cm high, slender, up to 1 cm thick, arising from a gelatinous egg-like stage which is oval, 2–3 cm long, whitish, with white root-like strands of mycelium. Stem whitish or pale buff, hollow, tapered above. Spore-bearing part conical, pointed, orange-red, covered with dark olive-brown, slimy spore mass

HABITAT: Around old stumps and logs in woods

SEASON: Summer–early winter

LOOKALIKES: *M. ravenelii*, only in hothouses

This is the only native species of the genus in Europe, though one or two others are introduced into hothouses. It is frequent in some areas, and easily recognised by the form and colour of the fruitbody. The genus *Mutinus* is similar to *Phallus*, but differs in having the spore-bearing head fused to the stem rather than forming a free, conical cap. *Mutinus ravenelii*, a North American species, now widespread in Europe in hothouses, is carmine-red and has a much stronger smell.

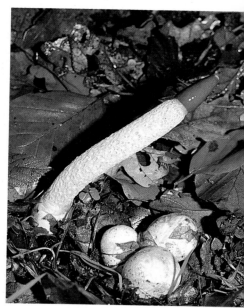

PHALLACEAE

Common Stinkhorn
Phallus impudicus

J	F	M	A	M	J
J	A	S	O	N	D

ID FACT FILE

FRUITBODY:
12–20 cm high,
arising from a
gelatinous egg-
like stage. Egg
3–6 cm long,
rounded, whitish,
with white, cord-
like mycelium.
Stem sponge-
like, hollow,
fragile, whitish,
with conical cap
attached only at
the top. Cap with
honeycomb-like
network of veins,
covered at first
by the slimy, foul
smelling, black-
ish-olive spore
mass

HABITAT: In soil
around stumps
in woods

SEASON:
Summer–autumn

LOOKALIKES:
P. hadriani has
pinkish eggs and
occurs in sand-
dunes

A common and well-known fungus often easily
located in woods by its strong, unpleasant
odour which attracts flies. Eggs of the
stinkhorn were once known as 'witches' eggs',
and the phallic shape of the expanded fruitbody has led to its use as an aphrodisiac.
Indeed, the species has a great deal of associated folklore, concerning either its smell or its
shape, and it is also popularly known as 'wood
witch'.

SARCOSCYPHACEAE

J	F	M	A	M	J
J	A	S	O	N	D

Scarlet Elf Cup
Sarcoscypha austriaca

ID FACT FILE

FRUITBODY:
Goblet-shaped, usually with distinct stalk, 1.5–5 cm across, margin often split, inner surface scarlet, outer surface whitish, felty

HABITAT: On dead wood amongst moss, gregarious

SEASON: Late winter–spring

LOOKALIKES: *S. coccinea*, distinguished only on microscopic characters, but apparently less common

This seems to have become more frequent in recent years, whereas the macroscopically identical *S. coccinea* has become scarcer. These are amongst the most attractive of the cup fungi; the bright scarlet fruitbodies, often in swarms amongst moss on dead branches, create an impressive sight in the winter months. In Britain, they have received a variety of folk names such as 'moss cups' and 'fairies' baths' and have been used as a table decoration.

OTIDEACEAE

J	F	M	A	M	J
J	A	S	O	N	D

Orange Peel Fungus
Aleuria aurantia

ID FACT FILE

FRUITBODY:
2–10 cm across, cup-shaped, later irregular to flattened, inner surface bright orange to orange-yellow, paler with age. Outer surface paler, whitish, minutely downy. Flesh thin, brittle

HABITAT: Gregarious, on bare soil of paths, etc.

SEASON: Late summer–late autumn

LOOKALIKES:
Melastiza chateri is similar in colour but smaller, usually densely clustered and with brownish margin

A well-known fungus, usually easily recognised by the orange, rather brittle, cup-shaped fruitbodies. These grow in clusters, usually on damp, bare soil, often on paths. Most larger cup-fungi, though very varied in form and colour, have been referred at some time to the genus *Peziza*, now much restricted in application, and have been popularly known as elf-cups. This species is also known as Great Orange Elf-cup.

OTIDEACEAE

Eye-lash Fungus
Scutellinia scutellata

ID FACT FILE

FRUITBODY: Disc-shaped, 3–7 mm across, reddish-orange, margin fringed with long, dark brown hairs. Hairs to 1 mm or more in length

HABITAT: Gregarious on damp soil and wet, rotten wood

SEASON: Mostly summer–autumn

LOOKALIKES: Other *Scutellinia* species, but most have shorter hairs

The commonest of the eye-lash fungi, often growing in swarms on wet, rotten wood. It is characterised particularly by the long marginal hairs but can be distinguished with certainty only by microscopic examination. Eye-lash fungi are almost worldwide in distribution and, although differing in size, colour and hair length, the various species can be very similar and it is the microscopic characters which are most important for identification.

PEZIZACEAE

Mortar Cup
Peziza cerea

ID FACT FILE

FRUITBODY:
2–6 cm across, cup-shaped to flattened, cream to pale yellowish, margin incurved when young. Inner surface smooth; outer surface paler, scurfy

HABITAT: On damp mortar, sand and old brickwork etc.

SEASON: All year

LOOKALIKES: Several other species of *Peziza*, which are more deeply coloured

Quite a common species, recognised by the substrate and by the consistently cream or pale yellowish fruitbodies. It is often seen around houses, fruiting on damp plaster and brickwork. Although it does no great harm, and will disappear when the area is dried, its presence in such places is generally indicative of undesirably damp conditions.

PEZIZACEAE

Stalked Wood Cup
Peziza micropus

ID FACT FILE

FRUITBODY:
2–6 cm across, cup-shaped to flattened, usually with a small stalk-like base and crenulate margin. Inner surface fawn or pale ochraceous, smooth. Outer surface paler, whitish, finely scurfy

HABITAT: On rotten wood, especially of elm and beech

SEASON: All year

LOOKALIKES: Several *Peziza* species, most of which grow on the ground, reliably distinguished only by microscopic characters

There are many species of *Peziza* in Europe, and their identification is usually critical and requires microscopic examination. This is perhaps the most common of the species that occur on wood. The colour and the finely toothed margin are characteristic, and there is usually a small stalk inserted under bark, hence the epithet *micropus*.

PEZIZACEAE

Bladder Cup

Peziza vesiculosa

ID FACT FILE

FRUITBODY: Irregularly cup-shaped, flesh thick, brittle, margin strongly inrolled when young, yellowish-buff throughout, 3–9 cm across, clustered. Inner surface often wrinkled and blistered. Outer surface scurfy

HABITAT: On manure and rich soil

SEASON: All year, but mostly summer–autumn

LOOKALIKES: Other *Peziza* species are thinner-fleshed

A common fungus, often met with in gardens where beds have been mulched with manure. It often grows in large quantities and is then an impressive sight. The thick, brittle flesh is characteristic as is the blistering of the inner surface which is commonly seen in mature fruitbodies due to the separation of the fertile layer from the underlying flesh. Inedible, even when cooked, and possibly poisonous.

PEZIZACEAE

| J | F | M | A | M | J |
| J | A | S | O | N | D |

Violet Bonfire Cup
Peziza violacea

ID FACT FILE

FRUITBODY:
Saucer-shaped,
1–3 cm across,
violaceous
throughout, outer
surface slightly
paler

HABITAT: Solitary
or in small
groups on burnt
ground

SEASON: All year,
especially
spring–early
summer

LOOKALIKES:
*Peziza pseudovi-
olacea*, distin-
guished on
microscopic
characters

One of a range of cup fungi to be found on
burnt ground, often growing in clusters. The
fruitbodies are often found growing amongst
the moss *Funaria*, and sometimes in company
with other cup fungi found on burnt ground, of
which more than 50 species are known in
Europe. It is fairly common but can be distinguished from a few other similarly coloured
species only by microscopic examination.

OTIDEACEAE

J	F	M	A	M	J
J	A	S	O	N	D

Common Hare's-ear
Otidea alutacea

This occurs in clusters in leaf litter, and is a fairly common species though quite easy to overlook. As with most species of *Otidea*, the cup is split down one side, but the opposite side in this species is not much elongated. The pale fawn colours are characteristic and it can usually be recognised in the field with experience, but microscopic examination is needed for certain identification.

ID FACT FILE

FRUITBODY: Cup-shaped, split down one side, often slightly higher on the other side, 2–6 cm across, 2–5 cm high. Inner surface pale fawn, smooth. Outer surface paler, finely scurfy

HABITAT: Soil, amongst leaf litter in woods

SEASON: Late summer–autumn

LOOKALIKES: Some other *Otidea* species, which are usually darker

OTIDEACEAE

J	F	M	A	M	J
J	A	S	O	N	D

Lemon Peel Fungus
Otidea onotica

ID FACT FILE

FRUITBODY: Ear-shaped, elongated on one side, 4–9 cm high, with short, whitish stalk. Inner surface yellowish with pink tints, more pronounced when dry. Outer surface yellowish, scurfy

HABITAT: On soil in woods

SEASON: Autumn

LOOKALIKES: A few other *Otidea* species, but these lack the pink tints

An uncommon species, similar in form to some other species of *Otidea*, but distinctive on account of its comparatively large and brightly coloured fruitbodies. In particular, the pink tinges on the inner surface, and the ear-like shape of the fruitbodies serve to distinguish it. It is usually found amongst leaf litter in deciduous woodland, and is particularly associated with oak.

OTIDEACEAE

Cedar Earth-cup
Geopora sumneriana

ID FACT FILE

FRUITBODY:
Developing
underground as
a hollow ball,
breaking surface
when mature and
splitting into
lobes at top,
deep cup-
shaped, 3–7 cm
across. Inner
surface cream,
outer surface
fibrous, brown-
ish, binding soil

HABITAT: Usually
under cedars

SEASON: Spring

LOOKALIKES:
G. foliacea
occurs in autumn
under other
trees. *G. sepulta*
is found deeply
buried in sandy
soil in autumn

A distinctive species, and one of the largest of
the genus. The cups are deeply sunk in the
ground, breaking the surface only at maturity,
and are almost always associated with cedar
trees in parks and gardens. Fruitbodies are
gregarious often occurring in large numbers.
Unlike most species of *Geopora* it occurs only
in the spring.

HELVELLACEAE

Ribbed Saddle
Helvella acetabulum

ID FACT FILE

FRUITBODY: Cup-shaped, with short furrowed stalk, cup 4–6 cm across, fawn brown to chestnut, outer surface paler, finely downy. Stalk 2–3 cm high, whitish, ribbed, ribs sharp-edged, extending onto base of cup

HABITAT: Woods, on sandy or calcareous soil

SEASON: Spring–summer

LOOKALIKES: *H. leucomelas* has shorter stalk and lacks ribs on cup base. *H. unicolor* has short stem and blunt ribs. *H. costifera* is less cupulate and pale grey-brown

One of several species of *Helvella* which are cup-shaped and were once referred to the genus *Paxina*. It is also known popularly as Vinegar Cup. This species is widespread in Europe, but rather localised and generally uncommon. It is poisonous when raw, although edible after being twice boiled, and is eaten in some parts of Europe.

HELVELLACEAE

Common White Saddle
Helvella crispa

ID FACT FILE

FRUITBODY:
Upright, 6–12 cm
high, cap saddle-
shaped, whitish
to cream or pale
fawn, underside
smooth, stalk
3–5 cm high,
1–2 cm thick,
deeply grooved
and ribbed

HABITAT: Woods,
copses

SEASON: Late
summer–autumn

LOOKALIKES: *H.
lacunosa* is dark
grey

One of the commonest of the saddle fungi,
widely distributed in the N hemisphere, occurring especially on sandy soil in forests and at
path edges. It is variable in size and shape, but
always with a whitish cap and white stem
which distinguish it from other species. The
fruitbodies are edible if well cooked but somewhat poisonous if eaten raw.

HELVELLACEAE

J	F	M	A	M	J
J	A	S	O	N	D

Elastic Saddle
Helvella elastica

ID FACT FILE

FRUITBODY:
Upright, 5–8 cm
high, head sad-
dle-shaped, fold-
ed and lobed,
often attached to
the stem, pale
greyish-brown,
1–3.5 cm
across, under-
side smooth.
Stalk whitish,
cylindric,
3–7 mm thick,
almost smooth,
not grooved

HABITAT: Woods,
path edges etc.

SEASON: Late sum-
mer–autumn

LOOKALIKES: *H.
latispora* has
whitish cap and
margin always
free from the
stem

This is one of several species of *Helvella* which
have a simple, non-grooved stem and a smooth
undersurface to the cap. The pale brown cap,
which has lobes attached to the stem, serves to
distinguish it. It can be found in both deciduous and coniferous woods, and is fairly common and widespread in Europe, and also
found in N America.

HELVELLACEAE

False Morel
Gyromitra esculenta

ID FACT FILE

FRUITBODY:
Stalked, fertile head reddish-brown, convoluted and brain-like in form, hollow, 4–10 cm across. Stem short, stout, up to 4 cm high, whitish or tinged cap colour, somewhat grooved, internally chambered

HABITAT: Sandy soil under conifers

SEASON: Spring

LOOKALIKES:
G. gigas is rare, more coarsely convoluted but distinguished with certainty only under the microscope. *G. infula*, in autumn, is smaller, less convoluted and more saddle-shaped

A distinctive species, frequent in some areas and perhaps now spreading in Britain. In Britain it is mostly northern in distribution, but is now found in parts of S England. The species contains monomethylhydrazine and is deadly poisonous if eaten raw. It can also be dangerous to inhale the fumes on cooking. Specimens should be boiled twice and the water discarded. When cooked properly, it is edible and good.

MORCHELLACEAE

Common Morel
Morchella esculenta

ID FACT FILE

FRUITBODY:
5–15 cm high,
stalked. Cap
yellow-brown,
ovate to round-
ed, honeycomb-
like, with
irregular sterile
ridges separating
fertile pits. Stem
often enlarged to
base, whitish,
scurfy, hollow

HABITAT: Often on
disturbed soil

SEASON: Spring

LOOKALIKES:
M. conica has
conical cap
with ridges
mostly parallel;
M. elata has
taller cap with
black vertical ribs

An excellent edible fungus, one of the most
sought-after fungi in spring. Large quantities
are sold in markets in some parts of Europe.
The fruitbodies can also be dried for use as a
flavouring. However, they should always be
well cooked before eating. This is a widespread
and fairly common species, but unpredictable
in appearance. It occurs especially on calcareous soil, often in disturbed places, but also in
woods.

LEOTIACEAE

| J | F | M | A | M | J |
| J | A | S | O | N | D |

Purple Jelly-cup
Ascocoryne sarcoides

ID FACT FILE

FRUITBODY: Of two kinds, both gelatinous and purple-red: early, asexual state irregular and convoluted, 1–3 cm across; accompanied or not by mature, sexual state 0.5–1 cm across, crowded, thick-fleshed, cup- or cushion-shaped, with narrowed base, smooth

HABITAT: On rotten stumps and logs, mostly of deciduous trees

SEASON: Late summer–winter

LOOKALIKES: *A. cylichnium* has larger fruitbodies, without an asexual state

A common and distinctive fungus, usually easy to recognise by its form, gelatinous texture, and colour. The asexual state, known as *Coryne dubia*, is lobed and irregular in form and may occur unaccompanied by the sexual stage. The latter, more cup-like and regular in form, is usually densely gregarious and may cover extensive areas of fallen trunks.

LEOTIACEAE

J	F	M	A	M	J
J	A	S	O	N	D

Black Bulgar
Bulgaria inquinans

ID FACT FILE

FRUITBODY: Gelatinous, rubbery, 1–3 cm across, at first subglobose, expanding. Fertile surface smooth, black. Outer surface brownish, scurfy. Spores black

HABITAT: On wood, especially of oak and beech

SEASON: Mainly autumn

LOOKALIKES: Black Brain Fungus (p.206) has papillate surface and white spores

Sometimes also known as Bachelor's Buttons, this is a distinctive fungus with black, rubbery flesh. The spores are also black, aiding distinction from Black Brain Fungus (p.206) which may look similar and is also common on oak. Fruitbodies occur on the bark of fallen trunks and logs, though the species is also sometimes a parasite on beech.

LEOTIACEAE

Green Wood-cup
Chlorosplenium aeruginascens

ID FACT FILE

FRUITBODY:
2–5 mm across, bright blue-green throughout, cup-shaped to irregular with short stalk, arising from green-stained wood

HABITAT: Gregarious, on rotten branches of oak, sometimes other trees

SEASON: Mostly autumn

LOOKALIKES:
C. aeruginosum has yellowish disc

The green-stained wood caused by this species is quite commonly found amongst woodland litter, though the fruitbodies, developed on barkless branches, are less often seen. This wood, known as 'green oak', has been used in inlay work, especially in the manufacture of Tunbridge Ware, a traditional English craft from the 19th century; the green colour resists fading much better than do most green dyes.

An example of Tunbridge Ware

LEOTIACEAE

J	F	M	A	M	J
J	A	S	O	N	D

Jelly Babies
Leotia lubrica

ID FACT FILE

FRUITBODY:
Upright, 2–5 cm high, gelatinous, club-shaped with convex, olive-yellow head 6–12 mm across. Stalk slightly tapered downwards, ochraceous, covered with minute greenish warts, becoming hollow

HABITAT: Damp areas in deciduous woods

SEASON: Late summer–autumn

LOOKALIKES: *Cudonia circinans*, pale yellow and not gelatinous

Fairly common, usually growing in clusters, and recognised by the capitate fruitbodies which have gelatinous flesh and yellow-green colours. The common name refers to the resemblance of the fruitbodies in form and texture to the popular sweets, but it is also known as Green Slime Fungus and Slippery Lizard Tuft. The fruitbodies are edible but cannot be recommended for culinary purposes.

LEOTIACEAE

J	F	M	A	M	J
J	A	S	O	N	D

Bog Beacon
Mitrula paludosa

ID FACT FILE

FRUITBODY:
Upright, narrowly
club-shaped,
2–5 cm high.
Fertile head
ovoid or cylindric,
smooth, bright
yellow-orange.
Stalk white,
moist, binding
algae and litter
at the base

HABITAT: Ditches
and wet places,
amongst rotting
leaves

SEASON:
Spring–early
summer

LOOKALIKES: None

The fruitbodies usually occur in swarms
amongst rotting leaves in wet places, mostly in
ditches, and are fairly common in late Spring.
It is an attractive species, the bright yellowish-
orange head being very distinctive and easy to
spot, hence the common name. Not poisonous,
but too small and tasteless, and quite worthless
as an edible species.

GEOGLOSSACEAE

J	F	M	A	M	J
J	A	S	O	N	D

Common Earth-tongue
Geoglossum cookeianum

ID FACT FILE

FRUITBODY: 5–8 cm high, upright, narrowly club-shaped or tongue-like, blackish, smooth, upper fertile part 3–5 mm wide, stalk distinct, about half the total height, cylindrical, 2 mm thick, minutely scurfy-scaly

HABITAT: In unimproved grassland or on sandy soil amongst moss

SEASON: Autumn–early winter

LOOKALIKES: Other *Geoglossum* species, only reliably distinguished on microscopic characters

One of several species of earth-tongues which are still locally frequent, but becoming less so as suitable habitats are lost. These species are usually easily recognisable as earth-tongues, but are individually difficult to distinguish without the aid of a microscope. *G. cookeianum* is widespread throughout Europe and is also found in North America.

GEOGLOSSACEAE

J	F	M	A	M	J
J	A	S	O	N	D

Hairy Earth-tongue
Trichoglossum hirsutum

ID FACT FILE

FRUITBODY:
Upright, tongue-shaped, 3–7 cm high, blackish, finely velvety throughout, stem slender, the fertile upper part usually rather flattened and variable in shape

HABITAT: In grass, sometimes in *Sphagnum*, on acid soils

SEASON: Late summer–late autumn

LOOKALIKES:
T. walteri differs on spore characters. *Geoglossum* species are similar but not velvety

Frequent in Europe and indeed almost world-wide in distribution. There are several common species of earth-tongue, amongst which the *Trichoglossum* species can be distinguished by their minutely velvety fruitbodies. This is due to stiff, thick-walled, dark brown, pointed hairs which occur over the entire surface of the fruitbody and are easy to see under a microscope.

CLAVICIPITACEAE

J	F	M	A	M	J
J	A	S	O	N	D

Ergot
Claviceps purpurea

ID FACT FILE

SCLEROTIUM:
Spindle-shaped,
1–1.5 cm long,
blackish, surface
furrowed. Fruit-
body formed on
overwintered
sclerotia, drum-
stick-shaped,
stalk slender,
fertile head sub-
globose 2–5 mm
across

HABITAT: Sclerotia
formed in the
flowerhead of
grasses

SEASON: Sclerotia
summer–autum;
fruitbody in
spring

LOOKALIKES: None

Sclerotia develop in the flowerheads of a wide
range of grasses and are very poisonous. In the
Middle Ages, poisoning due to eating infected
grain was common, and was known as 'Holy
Fire'. This disease is now called ergotism,
symptoms of which include gangrene and hallucinations, and may lead to death. However,
the drugs involved are now used for migraine
and other medical problems.

CLAVICIPITACEAE

Scarlet Caterpillar Fungus
Cordyceps militaris

ID FACT FILE

FRUITBODY:
2–4 cm high, bright orange, club shaped, fertile head with finely roughened surface; stalk paler, more yellowish

HABITAT: On dead larvae of noctuid moths buried in the soil

SEASON: Autumn

LOOKALIKES: None

The bright orange, upright fruitbodies, mostly found in pastures and open grassy areas, makes this a highly distinctive fungus. It is also one of the commonest of the European species of *Cordyceps* most of which occur on insects, though a few are found on underground truffle-like fruitbodies of *Elaphomyces*. It is a highly specialised parasite, like all *Cordyceps* species, which attacks and eventually kills the host caterpillar after it has burrowed into the soil to pupate.

XYLARIACEAE

| J | F | M | A | M | J |
| J | A | S | O | N | D |

Cramp-balls
Daldinia concentrica

ID FACT FILE

FRUITBODY:
Hemispherical,
2–10 cm across,
reddish-brown at
first, soon black-
ish. Surface
hard, shiny.
Flesh with dis-
tinct concentric
greyish-white and
black zones.
Spores brown

HABITAT: On dead
wood of ash,
birch and some-
times other trees

SEASON: All year

LOOKALIKES: *D.
vernicosa* has
soft flesh and is
usually on burnt
gorse

Carrying the fruitbodies in the pocket was once
regarded as an effective safeguard against
cramp. It is also known as King Alfred's Cakes as
the black, carbonaceous fruitbodies have the
appearance of being burned. Fruitbodies may
also occur on burnt trunks, but should not be
confused with the similar but softer-fleshed and
smaller *Daldinia vernicosa* which is less common
and often found on burnt gorse. The species
causes a white, mottled rot with black speckling
which, in ash, is known as 'calico wood'.

XYLARIACEAE

Birch Wood-wart
Hypoxylon multiforme

ID FACT FILE

FRUITBODY:
Cushion-like,
somewhat elon-
gated or irregular
in shape,
2–3 cm across,
larger when
fused together,
hard and car-
bonised, surface
reddish at first,
later blackish,
roughened.
Spores black

HABITAT: On dead
stumps and
branches of birch
and alder

SEASON: All year

LOOKALIKES: Other
red *Hypoxylon*
species differ in
shape and host

Common in many areas, usually on birch, but occasionally on alder or other trees. The fruit-bodies are commonly developed on bark of dead branches, growing out through the lenticels, but also occur on bare wood. The flask-shaped spore-bearing structures, or perithecia, which are embedded in the upper part of the fruitbody, are comparatively large, almost 1 mm across, and give a distinct, undulating outline to the surface.

XYLARIACEAE

Candle-snuff Fungus
Xylaria hypoxylon

ID FACT FILE

FRUITBODY:
Upright, to 7 cm
high; when imma-
ture branched,
antler-like, flat-
tened, stalk
black, hairy,
upper part white
and powdery.
Mature, sexual,
fruitbody black
throughout,
unbranched,
pointed, upper
fertile part thick-
er, cylindric,
roughened

HABITAT: On dead
stumps and logs

SEASON: All year

LOOKALIKES: Very
distinctive. *X. car-
pophila* is much
more slender
and occurs on
beech mast

A common and readily recognisable species
occuring on various kinds of dead wood, and
reported to have a mycelium which is luminous. The whitish, stag-horn-like fruitbodies of
the conidial state are said to resemble snuffed-
out candle wicks. These and the black sexual
fruitbodies occur commonly together on the
same stump or log. A related and similar but
more slender species, *X. carpophila*, occurs on
fallen beech mast.

XYLARIACEAE

Dead-man's Fingers
Xylaria polymorpha

ID FACT FILE

FRUITBODY:
3–8 cm high,
1–2 cm wide,
stalked, club-
shaped, often
irregular in form,
flattened and
contorted, black,
surface rough-
ened with minute
warts. Flesh firm,
tough, white.
Spores black

HABITAT: On old
stumps of
deciduous trees,
especially beech

SEASON: All year

LOOKALIKES: *X. longipes* is more
cylindric and
grows on *Acer*

The fruitbodies, in the form of black, finger-
like clubs, arise from rotten logs and stumps
and it is not difficult to see how the popular
name was derived. It is sometimes also known
as Devil's Fingers. This is quite a common and
widely distributed species, though because of
its dull colour and its occurrence in shady
wooded areas it often tends to be rather
inconspicuous.

GLOSSARY

Adnate of gill or tubes, with broad attachment to the stipe

Adnexed of gills or tubes, with narrow attachment to stipe

Agaric A mushroom or toadstool, a member of the order Agaricales

Cap The part of the fruitbody, especially in agarics, which bears the spore-producing tissue

Chlamydospore A special type of asexual, single-celled, usually thick-walled spore

Clavate Cup-shaped

Crowded of gills, closely-spaced

Cuticle The outer layer or 'skin', usually the cap of an agaric

Cortina Cobweb-like veil that covers the gills, connecting the cap margin to the stipe

Decurrent of gills or tubes, broadly attached to the stipe and extending down it

Deliquescent Dissolving into liquid at maturity

Distant of gills, widely-spaced, not crowded

Fibril A very small fibre

Fibrillose Bearing fibrils

Free of gills or tubes, not attached to the stipe

Fruitbody The structure that bears the spore-producing tissue

Hygrophanous Water-soaked, becoming opaque and paler during drying; usually referring to the cap of an agaric

Hypha Microscopic, thread-like structure of which the mycelium and fruitbodies of all fungi are composed

Mycelium Aggregation of hyphae

Mycorrhiza Specialised symbiotic relationship between the mycelium of a fungus and the root of the host plant

Parasite An organism that derives its nutrients from living host tissue, supplying nothing in return

Partial veil Tissue that protects the gills in agarics, connecting the cap margin and stipe

Pellicle Detachable, skin-like layer on the cap of an agaric

Peridole Small, egg-shaped structure which contains the spores in Bird's-nest fungi

Pores The ends of the tubes in polypores and boletes, as seen in surface view

Resupinate Growing effused on the substratum, skin-like

Rhizomorph Root-like strand of mycelium, usually with dark rind and white flesh

Ring Remains of the partial veil on the stem

Saprophyte An organism that derives its nutrients from dead plant or animal remains

Sclerotium Sterile mass of modified, thick-walled hyphae that acts as a resting stage

Sinuate of gills or tubes, having a notch or S-shape at the lower edge where they join the stem

Spore Reproductive unit of fungi

Stipe The stem of a fungus

Striate Finely grooved

Tubes The spore-bearing tissue found in polypores and boletes

Umbilicate of the cap of an agaric, having a small, central depression

Umbo Central raised area or boss, usually of the cap of an agaric

Veil Protective, usually membranous tissue that covers all or part of the developing fruitbody of an agaric

Volva Remains of the partial veil, forming a usually sac-like structure at the stipe base of an agaric

INDEX

● Collins

If you have enjoyed this book, why not have a look at some of the other titles in the WILD GUIDE series?

Birds	0-00-717792-5
Wild Flowers	0-00-717793-3
Insects	0-00-717795-X
Night Sky	0-00-717790-9
Night Sky Starfinder	0-00-717791-7
Weather	0-00-716072-0
Seashore	0-00-716071-2
Garden Birds	0-00-717789-5
Butterflies	0-00-719151-0
Trees	0-00-719152-9
Rocks and Minerals	0-00-717794-1
British Wildlife	0-00-719172-3

Also from Collins:

How to Idenitfy Edible Mushrooms
by Patrick Harding, Tony Lyon and Gill Tomblin
0-00-219984-X

To order any of these titles please call **0870 787 1732**.

For further information about Collins books visit our website: **www.collins.co.uk**